SpringerBriefs in Information Systems

Series Editor

Jörg Becker, Münster, Germany

SpringerBriefs present concise summaries of cutting-edge research and practical applications across a wide spectrum of fields. Featuring compact volumes of 50 to 125 pages, the series covers a range of content from professional to academic. Typical topics might include: A timely report of state-of-the art analytical techniques, a bridge between new research results, as published in journal articles, and a contextual literature review, a snapshot of a hot or emerging topic, an in-depth case study or practical example, a presentation of core concepts that students must understand in order to make independent contributions. SpringerBriefs in Information Systems showcase emerging theory, empirical research, and practical application in all subcategories of information systems and related fields, from a global author community. Briefs are characterized by fast, global electronic dissemination, standard publishing contracts, standardized manuscript preparation and formatting guidelines, and expedited production schedules.

Jürgen Anke

Smart Service Innovation

An Ecosystem Perspective on Organization,
Design, and Assessment

 Springer

Jürgen Anke (ID)
Faculty of Computer Science/Mathematics
HTW Dresden University of Applied Sciences
Dresden, Germany

ISSN 2192-4929   ISSN 2192-4937   (electronic)
SpringerBriefs in Information Systems
ISBN 978-3-031-43769-4   ISBN 978-3-031-43770-0   (eBook)
https://doi.org/10.1007/978-3-031-43770-0

This Springer imprint is published by the registered company Springer Nature Switzerland AG
The registered company address is: Gewerbestrasse 11, 6330 Cham, Switzerland

Paper in this product is recyclable.

Foreword

Digital transformation has profoundly changed the business models and processes in numerous industries. These developments are based on the ubiquity of networked information technologies that capture data at the points of origin and make it available for other purposes at diverse points of use. In particular, the technologies of the Internet of Things (IoT) have enabled data-based business models, which represent combinations of physical objects and usage-based adaptive services with a high level of personalization in relation to their users. Well-known examples of such smart services include pay-per-use applications in the sharing economy as well as predictive applications in the field of maintenance or energy management. Contrary to traditional digital services (e.g., weather, booking, or banking service), smart services are systems of services that combine different complementary competencies. For example, a smart mobility service comprises the physical vehicles and the fleet operators as well as the providers of billing, navigation, and digital platform services.

Two main implications result from the nature of smart services as service systems: On the one hand, such solutions have a high structural complexity due to the networking of several heterogeneous actors. On the other hand, due to their dynamic properties, they have a high degree of uncertainty with respect to the reliable interplay of all elements during operations that follows from the design phase. In general, a variety of methodologies exist that could be used to design and manage smart services. These originate from software engineering (e.g., UML, Scrum), process management (e.g., BPMN, business process redesign) as well as business modeling (e.g., e3value, canvas models). Although service systems engineering methods have emerged in the engineering discipline, even these approaches only contribute individual aspects to the identification, design, and operation of smart services. This gap represents the motivation of the post-doctoral thesis on smart service innovation presented by Jürgen Anke, which is summarized in this book.

Smart service innovation offers a comprehensive framework for understanding the complexities and uncertainties involved in smart service design and management. On the one hand, it comprises the process of creating a network of partners for a smart service and the implementation of the developed smart service on the other. In the tradition of the business information systems and engineering discipline, the smart service innovation framework recognizes the multidimensional nature and distinguishes multiple design aspects on three different design levels. This led to an impressive collection of artifacts, which are not only consistently rooted in prior knowledge (i.e., the literature). In addition, the artifacts are linked with various use cases (e.g., for fleet management) that illustrate their use in practice. The probability of being applied in practice might also benefit from the reuse of many existing methodologies. Rather than proposing a new comprehensive, and possibly also complex, methodology, the smart service innovation framework diligently links methodological elements from the existing approaches mentioned above.

Overall, the book represents a rich and impressive contribution to the highly topical subject area of smart services, which is equally relevant from both a scientific and applied perspective. It represents an impressive and successful example of how scientific rigor and practical relevance may be balanced toward a result that deems broad dissemination in both worlds.

Faculty of Economics and Management   Rainer Alt
Science
Leipzig University
Leipzig, Germany

Acknowledgments

This book is the result of research I have conducted in recent years on the fascinating topic of smart service innovation. It has been a journey in which I had the pleasure and privilege to collaborate with many inspiring people who helped me to bring this research endeavor forward. Therefore, I would like to particularly thank Jens Pöppelbuß, Martin Ebel, Andreas Zolnowski, Stefan Wellsandt, Julian Krenge, and Fabian Richter for their valuable input and vivid discussions. I enjoyed working with you very much! I would also like to thank the numerous experts who agreed to support my research as interview partners or test subjects.

A special thanks go to Rainer Alt, who accompanied me throughout the work and supported me with words and deeds. Thanks a lot for your guidance!

This book and its underlying research papers would not have been possible without my family's ongoing support and love, who have been very understanding of my efforts to complete this work. Thank you very much!

Dresden, July 2023

Jürgen Anke

Contents

Abbreviations

ADR   Action Design Research
AI   Artificial Intelligence
B2C   Business-to-Consumer
BM   Business Model
BMC   Business Model Canvas
BMDT   Business Model Design Tool
BMI   Business Model Innovation
BOL   Beginning-of-Life
BPMN   Business Process Model and Notation
CPS   Cyber-Physical Systems
DDBM   Data-driven Business Model
DIN   Deutsches Institut für Normung
DSL   Domain-specific Language
DSM   Digital service specific methods
DSR   Design Science Research
DSRM   Design Science Research Methodology
EOL   End-of-Life
GPM   General-Purpose Methods
IEC   International Electrotechnical Commission
IoT   Internet of Things
IS   Information Systems
ISO   International Organization for Standardization
IT   Information Technology
LML   Lifecycle Modelling Language
MBSE   Model-based Systems Engineering
ME   Method Engineering
MOL   Middle-of-Life
MQTT   Message Queuing Telemetry Transport
MVP   Minimum Viable Product
OPC-UA   Open Platform Communications Unified Architecture
PLM   Product Lifecycle Management

PSS	Product-Service System
RQ	Research Question
SBMC	Service Business Model Canvas
SDL	Service-Dominant Logic
SE	Service Engineering
SEM	Service engineering methods
SME	Situational Method Engineering
SSE	Service Systems Engineering
SSI	Smart Service Innovation
SysML	System Modelling Language
UCD	User-centered Design Methods
UI	User Interface
UML	Unified Modelling Language
UX	User Experience

Chapter 1
Introduction

1.1 Motivation

The ongoing digital transformation is "a process that aims to improve an entity by triggering significant changes to its properties through combinations of information, computing, communication, and connectivity technologies" (Vial 2019: 118). It provides organizations of all industries ample opportunities for creating a competitive advantage, including innovative smart service offerings. Examples of smart services can be found in consumer markets where car makers connect vehicles with digital platforms to analyze driving behavior based on sensor data, schedule workshop appointments, provide usage-based insurance, or give feedback on driving behavior (Beverungen et al. 2019b; Husnjak et al. 2015). In the industrial domain, manufacturers innovate by combining digitally connected machines and equipment with value propositions like predictive maintenance, remote service and control, fleet management, and pay-per-use models (Herterich et al. 2015; Heuchert et al. 2020).

Smart service innovation (SSI) inherently reflects the process of digital transformation, as it utilizes digital technologies such as the Internet of Things (IoT), big data, artificial intelligence (AI), and cloud computing as enablers of new value-creating and revenue-generating opportunities (Demirkan et al. 2015; Parida et al. 2019; Sjödin et al. 2020b) that change the value propositions and value creation processes of organizations (Vial 2019; Wessel et al. 2021). SSI establishes smart service systems, which rely on physical objects with computation, data storage, sensors, actuators, and networking capability (Porter and Heppelmann 2014). Such smart products serve as boundary objects between actors of the service system (e.g., service consumers and providers) and enable or facilitate mutual value creation (Allmendinger and Lombreglia 2005; Beverungen et al. 2019a; National Science Foundation 2014).

However, creating novel smart service offerings is challenging in practice, mainly due to the associated complexity and uncertainty. This may lead to situations described as *digital paradox*, in which "increasing revenues from digital services

J. Anke, *Smart Service Innovation*, SpringerBriefs in Information Systems,
https://doi.org/10.1007/978-3-031-43770-0_1

fail to deliver greater profits because of rampant cost increases" (Sjödin et al. 2020a: 479). Some of the challenges identified are the lack of skills for digital innovation and solution design, technical interoperability problems, the management of multiple stakeholders, and unclear regulations regarding privacy and data ownership (Bonamigo and Frech 2020; Ebel 2021; Klein et al. 2018; Wolf et al. 2020).

Smart service innovation has become a central topic for information systems (IS) research over the last years (Beverungen et al. 2019b; Yang et al. 2021) with links to many other disciplines, including services marketing (Wuenderlich et al. 2015), industrial marketing management (Sjödin et al. 2020a; Sklyar et al. 2019), innovation management (Maglio and Lim 2016), and industrial engineering (Rabe et al. 2018). The information systems discipline is particularly suitable for studying smart service systems' systematic development due to its interdisciplinary nature (Böhmann et al. 2014). In this context, the "service systems engineering" (SSE) approach goes beyond traditional service engineering "towards systemic, interactive and collaborative service innovation based on advances in IT" (Böhmann et al. 2014) that adopts the ideas of service systems (Beverungen et al. 2018; Maglio et al. 2009) and service ecosystems (Vargo and Lusch 2016, 2017; Vink et al. 2021). Höckmayr and Roth (2017) have formulated requirements for SSE methods that include, among others, the imperative to "address larger constellations within which multiple actors become joined over time and space" and to "acknowledge the role of knowledge and skills applied by various actors" in service innovation (Höckmayr and Roth 2017). Referring to digital transformation more broadly, Alt (2019) similarly calls for methodologies that cover an ecosystem-wide perspective and integrate aspects of business and technological change. There is little empirical research on performances by individual actors within such multi-actor settings, which has been identified as an open research issue in digital transformation (Vial 2019).

The existing SSE design knowledge for the systematic development of service systems includes reference process models with phases, activities, and methods to guide the development of service systems (Beverungen et al. 2018, 2019a, b; Jussen et al. 2019). Studies show that organizations already employ iterative and agile ways of working to deal with complexity and reduce uncertainty, but current SSE methods lack support for multi-actor settings (Sjödin et al. 2020a). Furthermore, the set of SSE methods is limited and should be extended through methods from disciplines such as business model innovation, user-centered design, and software engineering to cater for the various design tasks in SSI (Holler et al. 2018). During the design of service systems in the various stages, an ongoing assessment can improve the quality of service concepts (Turetken et al. 2019) and their business models (Tesch et al. 2017). However, such assessments have little support (Szopinski et al. 2019).

The purpose of this book is to address these gaps by focusing on three main topics: (1) *organization*, i.e., the involvement, contributions, and activities of different actors in SSI, (2) *design*, i.e., the suitability and combination of existing methods for SSI, and (3) *assessment*, i.e., the development of new methods for the assessment of service systems during their design. The research approach combines empirical research and design science approaches, including expert interviews,

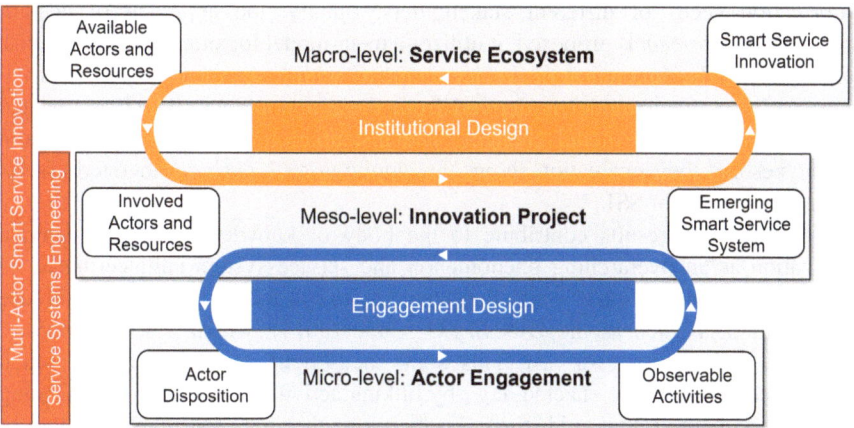

Fig. 1.1 Multi-level framework for smart service innovation

qualitative analysis, case studies, conceptual modeling, prototyping, and experiments to evaluate artifacts.

To capture the empirical phenomena and organize the research findings, a multi-level framework perspective on smart service innovation (Fig. 1.1) is established based on the work of Storbacka et al. (2016) and Grotherr et al. (2018). It describes the reconfiguration of resources by multiple actors in a service ecosystem toward a new value proposition on the macro-level. Depending on the need for different resources, suitable actors are involved (institutional design cycle). The collaboration of involved actors is facilitated by projects, which represent the meso-level of this framework. Projects can be understood as a configuration of actors, resources, and the rules of engagement. They form the context in which individual actors collaborate, e.g., by establishing project management mechanisms, enacting a development process, and distributing work. The establishment and adaption of the project create the context for the performances of individual actors (engagement design cycle). At the micro-level, actors conduct their work using methods representing the knowledge and skills they consider suitable. The created work products are integrated into a smart service system as continuously evolving project results at the meso-level, which in turn enables the desired new value proposition for the target customers at the macro-level.

Contributions regarding the *organization* include a set of ecosystem roles that actors may assume, and innovation patterns, which describe typical configurations of actors and roles. In addition, a model that relates individual actors' performed activities to reducing uncertainty at the project level is proposed. Regarding the *design*, methods for developing and documenting different aspects of the service system are gathered along with various challenges in designing services. It is shown that combining methods from different disciplines is both feasible and valuable in SSI. To capture the variety of service system elements and their dependencies, the Lifecycle Modeling Language (LML) has been found to be suitable to fulfill the information needs of different stakeholders. Finally, the approach of design-integrated *assessment* is proposed. It utilizes a meta-model for smart service systems, which allows the annotation of service elements with assessment-related information. An assessment model is derived from these annotations, which is updated whenever the service model changes. The instantiation of these models in tool prototypes and their evaluation shows that applying such design-integrated assessment is beneficial in SSI.

The presented results contribute to the body of knowledge in smart service innovation as an overarching phenomenon and service system engineering as an emerging discipline. Specifically, they can be used to enhance existing reference process models, such as the DIN SPEC 33453 (2019), which describes phases, activities, and methods for SSI. This book sheds light on the context in which such process models are enacted, e.g., by linking activities to actors and indicating the required methods that guide them. Furthermore, the range of suitable methods to support these activities is extended. For practitioners, this research provides valuable insights for the organization of smart service innovation. On an operational level, the enactment of service innovation processes is supported by a better understanding of involved actors, their roles, and activities, as well as by suitable methods for service design and assessment. Strategically, the presented results might assist in evaluating external dependencies and planning skill development within one's own organization.

1.2 Research Objectives and Research Questions

Service systems engineering (SSE) as an emerging discipline "seeks to advance knowledge on models, methods, and artifacts that enable or support the engineering of service systems" (Böhmann et al. 2014). This work aims to contribute to SSE by providing empirical evidence from real-world projects on the organizational setup and suitable methods for designing and assessing smart services. Within this goal, the three research objectives with associated research questions are defined as follows:

Objective 1: Understand the organizational setup of SSI. The complexity of smart service systems and the variety of required elements for such systems require various competencies, which are typically not found within a single organization. Additionally, innovation processes are beset with multiple types of uncertainty. For instance, customer requirements are often unclear and must be discovered. Therefore, it can be assumed that SSI requires the involvement of multiple actors (Lusch and Nambisan 2015). This aligns with the S-D logic perspective of innovation as the reconfiguration of resources in an ecosystem of actors. Understanding which resources they contribute, which activities they perform, and how they collaboratively reduce uncertainty provides the context for enacting SSI reference process models. Furthermore, a better understanding of multi-actor SSI illustrates the complexity and need for collaboration in such innovation projects. For the first research objective, the following research questions (RQ) are defined:

- RQ 1.1: Which roles are assumed by the actors involved in SSI?
- RQ 1.2: Which actor-role constellations can be identified that reflect recurring SSI patterns?
- RQ 1.3: How does the involvement of actors change over time?
- RQ 1.4: How do involved actors reduce uncertainty in SSI projects?

Objective 2: Evaluate the suitability of existing methods for SSI. Depending on its role, any actor responsible for certain activities in SSI must find a suitable approach to perform these activities within the project constraints of quality, cost, and time. This requires a suitable development process and project management approach. While smart service systems have specific traits, other disciplines have already addressed the problem of designing complex systems under uncertainty. To avoid re-inventing the wheel, it is worthwhile to evaluate if existing methods, including models, techniques, and notations, are suitable for SSI and how they can be combined meaningfully (Marx et al. 2020). The variety of methods leads to a fragmentation of work products that impedes establishing an integrated view of the emerging service system. A promising solution for this issue is the Lifecycle Modeling Language, which is evaluated regarding its suitability for SSI. Within the second objective, the following RQs are defined:

- RQ 2.1: Which methods for service design are applied in practice for SSI?
- RQ 2.2: Which challenges can be identified with applied SSI means in practice?
- RQ 2.3: How can methods from different disciplines be combined to support SSI?
- RQ 2.4: Which information needs in the lifecycle of smart service systems can be fulfilled with the Lifecycle Modeling Language?

Objective 3: Develop methods for design-integrated assessment in SSI. Creativity methods are employed to identify innovative value propositions for smart services that typically result in many ideas. Companies should assess their financial impact during the design process, to select to most promising ones for further elaboration and justify the required funding. Furthermore, research has found that assessing service business models during their development improves their overall quality (Turetken et al. 2019). Currently, the research on how to integrate the assessment of service concepts into development activities is sparse. Therefore, the third research objective aims to develop new methods for the design-integrated assessment of smart service ideas and their business models within SSI. The following two RQs address this research objective:

- RQ 3.1: How can smart services be financially assessed?
- RQ 3.2: How can service business models be assessed?

1.3   Book Structure

This book consists of eight chapters. Chapter 2 introduces service-dominant logic, smart service systems, and multi-actor smart service innovation as foundational concepts and theories. Chapter 3 covers current approaches to the systematic development of service systems. Chapter 4 provides a summary of the research approach and the methods that were applied to address the research questions stated above. The key findings are presented in Chap. 5, which are organized along the main aspects of SSI covered in this book, namely organization, design, and assessment. The discussion of these results in Chap. 6 covers theoretical contributions, limitations, managerial implications, and directions for future research. The book closes with a conclusion in Chap. 7.

References

DIN SPEC. (2019). *DIN SPEC 33453 Entwicklung digitaler Dienstleistungssysteme.* DIN.

Allmendinger, G., & Lombreglia, R. (2005). Four strategies for the age of smart services. *Harvard Business Review, 83,* 131.

Alt, R. (2019). Electronic markets on digital transformation methodologies. *Electronic Markets, 29,* 307–313. https://doi.org/10.1007/s12525-019-00370-x

Beverungen, D., Lüttenberg, H., & Wolf, V. (2018). Recombinant service systems engineering. *Business and Information Systems Engineering, 60,* 377–391. https://doi.org/10.1007/s12599-018-0526-4

Beverungen, D., Müller, O., Matzner, M., Mendling, J., & Vom Brocke, J. (2019a). Conceptualizing smart service systems. *Electronic Markets, 29,* 7–18. https://doi.org/10.1007/s12525-017-0270-5

Beverungen, D., Breidbach, C. F., Pöppelbuß, J., & Tuunainen, V. K. (2019b). Smart service systems: An interdisciplinary perspective. *Information Systems Journal, 29,* 1201–1206. https://doi.org/10.1111/isj.12275

Böhmann, T., Leimeister, J. M., & Möslein, K. (2014). Service systems engineering. *Business and Information Systems Engineering, 6,* 73–79. https://doi.org/10.1007/s12599-014-0314-8

Bonamigo, A., & Frech, C. G. (2020). Industry 4.0 in services: Challenges and opportunities for value co-creation. *Journal of Services Marketing, 35,* 412. https://doi.org/10.1108/JSM-02-2020-0073

Demirkan, H., Bess, C., Spohrer, J., Rayes, A., Allen, D., & Moghaddam, Y. (2015). Innovations with smart service systems: Analytics, big data, cognitive assistance, and the internet of everything. *Communications of the Association for Information Systems, 37.*

Ebel, M. (2021). Design-driven smart service innovation. In *AMCIS 2021 Proceedings.*

Grotherr, C., Semmann, M., & Böhmann, T. (2018). Using microfoundations of value co-creation to guide service systems design–A multilevel design framework. In *Thirty Ninth International Conference on Information Systems.*

Herterich, M., Uebernickel, F., & Brenner, W. (2015). The impact of cyber-physical systems on industrial services in manufacturing. *Procedia CIRP, 30,* 323–328. https://doi.org/10.1016/j.procir.2015.02.110

Heuchert, M., Verhoeven, Y., Cordes, A.-K., & Becker, J. (2020). Smart service systems in manufacturing: An investigation of theory and practice. In T. Bui (Ed.), *Proceedings of the 53rd Hawaii International Conference on System Sciences.* Hawaii International Conference on System Sciences.

Höckmayr, B., & Roth, A. (2017). Design of a Method for service systems engineering in the digital age. In Y. J. Kim, R. Agarwal, & J. K. Lee (Eds.), *Proceedings of the International Conference on Information Systems–Transforming Society with Digital Innovation, ICIS 2017, Seoul, South Korea*. Association for Information Systems.

Holler, M., Herterich, M., Dremel, C., Uebernickel, F., & Brenner, W. (2018). Towards a method compendium for the development of digitised products–findings from a case study. *IJPLM, 11*, 131. https://doi.org/10.1504/IJPLM.2018.092825

Husnjak, S., Peraković, D., Forenbacher, I., & Mumdziev, M. (2015). Telematics system in usage based motor insurance. *Procedia Engineering, 100*, 816–825. https://doi.org/10.1016/j.proeng.2015.01.436

Jussen, P., Kuntz, J., Senderek, R., & Moser, B. (2019). Smart service engineering. *Procedia CIRP, 83*, 384–388. https://doi.org/10.1016/j.procir.2019.04.089

Klein, M. M., Biehl, S. S., & Friedli, T. (2018). Barriers to smart services for manufacturing companies–An exploratory study in the capital goods industry. *Journal of Business & Industrial Marketing, 33*, 846–856. https://doi.org/10.1108/JBIM-10-2015-0204

Lusch, R. F., & Nambisan, S. (2015). Service innovation: A service-dominant logic perspective. *MIS Quarterly, 39*, 155–175.

Maglio, P. P., & Lim, C.-H. (2016). Innovation and big data in smart service systems. *Journal of Innovation Management, 4*, 11–21.

Maglio, P. P., Vargo, S. L., Caswell, N., & Spohrer, J. (2009). The service system is the basic abstraction of service science. *Information Systems and e-Business Management, 7*, 395–406. https://doi.org/10.1007/s10257-008-0105-1

Marx, E., Pauli, T., Fielt, E., & Matzner, M. (2020). From services to smart services: Can service engineering methods get smarter as well? In *15th International Conference on Wirtschaftsinformatik*.

National Science Foundation. (2014). *Partnerships for innovation: building innovation capacity* (PFI:BIC). https://www.nsf.gov/pubs/2013/nsf13587/nsf13587.htm

Parida, V., Sjödin, D., & Reim, W. (2019). Reviewing literature on digitalization, business model innovation, and sustainable industry: Past achievements and future promises. *Sustainability, 11*, 391. https://doi.org/10.3390/su11020391

Porter, M. E., & Heppelmann, J. E. (2014). How smart, connected products are transforming competition. *Harvard Business Review, 92*, 64–88.

Rabe, M., Kühn, A., Dumitrescu, R., Mittag, T., Schneider, M., & Gausemeier, J. (2018). Impact of smart services to current value networks. *Journal of Mechanical Engineering, 5*, 1–11.

Sjödin, D., Parida, V., Kohtamäki, M., & Wincent, J. (2020a). An agile co-creation process for digital servitization: A micro-service innovation approach. *Journal of Business Research, 112*, 478–491. https://doi.org/10.1016/j.jbusres.2020.01.009

Sjödin, D., Parida, V., Jovanovic, M., & Visnjic, I. (2020b). Value creation and value capture alignment in business model innovation: A process view on outcome-based business models. *Journal of Product Innovation Management, 37*, 158–183. https://doi.org/10.1111/jpim.12516

Sklyar, A., Kowalkowski, C., Tronvoll, B., & Sörhammar, D. (2019). Organizing for digital servitization: A service ecosystem perspective. *Journal of Business Research, 104*, 450–460. https://doi.org/10.1016/j.jbusres.2019.02.012

Storbacka, K., Brodie, R. J., Böhmann, T., Maglio, P. P., & Nenonen, S. (2016). Actor engagement as a microfoundation for value co-creation. *Journal of Business Research, 69*, 3008–3017. https://doi.org/10.1016/j.jbusres.2016.02.034

Szopinski, D., Schoormann, T., John, T., Knackstedt, R., & Kundisch, D. (2019). Software tools for business model innovation: Current state and future challenges. *Electronic Markets, 60*, 469. https://doi.org/10.1007/s12525-018-0326-1

Tesch, J. F., Brillinger, A.-S., & Bilgeri, D. (2017). Internet of things business model innovation and the stage-gate process: An exploratory analysis. *International Journal of Innovation Management, 21*, 1740002. https://doi.org/10.1142/S1363919617400023

Turetken, O., Grefen, P., Gilsing, R., & Adali, O. E. (2019). Service-dominant business model design for digital innovation in smart mobility. *Business and Information Systems Engineering, 61*, 9–29. https://doi.org/10.1007/s12599-018-0565-x

Vargo, S. L., & Lusch, R. F. (2016). Institutions and axioms: An extension and update of service-dominant logic. *Journal of the Academy of Marketing Science, 44*, 5–23. https://doi.org/10.1007/s11747-015-0456-3

Vargo, S. L., & Lusch, R. F. (2017). Service-dominant logic 2025. *International Journal of Research in Marketing, 34*, 46–67. https://doi.org/10.1016/j.ijresmar.2016.11.001

Vial, G. (2019). Understanding digital transformation: A review and a research agenda. *The Journal of Strategic Information Systems, 28*, 118–144. https://doi.org/10.1016/j.jsis.2019.01.003

Vink, J., Koskela-Huotari, K., Tronvoll, B., Edvardsson, B., & Wetter-Edman, K. (2021). Service ecosystem design: Propositions, process model, and future research agenda. *Journal of Service Research, 24*, 168–186. https://doi.org/10.1177/1094670520952537

Wessel, L., Baiyere, A., Ologeanu-Taddei, R., Cha, J., & Blegind Jensen, T. (2021). Unpacking the difference between digital transformation and IT-enabled organizational transformation. *Journal of the Association for Information Systems, 22*, 102–129. https://doi.org/10.17705/1jais.00655

Wolf, V., Franke, A., Bartelheimer, C., & Beverungen, D. (2020). Establishing smart service systems is a challenge: A case study on pitfalls and implications. In N. Gronau, M. Heine, K. Poustcchi, & H. Krasnova (Eds.), *WI2020 community tracks* (pp. 103–119). GITO Verlag.

Wuenderlich, N. V., Heinonen, K., Ostrom, A. L., Patricio, L., Sousa, R., Voss, C., & Lemmink, J. G. (2015). "Futurizing" smart service: Implications for service researchers and managers. *Journal of Services Marketing, 29*, 442–447. https://doi.org/10.1108/JSM-01-2015-0040

Yang, Y.-C., Ying, H., Jin, Y., Cheng, H. K., & Liang, T.-P. (2021). Special issue editorial: Information systems research in the age of smart services. *Journal of the Association for Information Systems, 22*, 579–590.

Chapter 2
Conceptual Background

2.1 Smart Service Systems

In service science, a *service system* is defined "as value-co-creation configurations of people, technology, value propositions connecting internal and external service systems, and shared information (e.g., language, laws, measures, and methods)" (Maglio & Spohrer, 2008: 18). Service systems, e.g., individuals and organizations, can be combined to composite service systems to form higher-level value co-creation relationships and alliances, i.e., they can be nested and overlap. Service systems are dynamic as they compose, recompose, and decompose over time (Maglio et al., 2009; Vargo & Akaka, 2012).

Digital technologies enable novel service systems as operant resources such as information, skills, and knowledge can be combined and exchanged in new ways that create value for the involved actors (Barrett et al., 2015; Edvardsson & Tronvoll, 2013; Nambisan, 2013; Sklyar et al., 2019; Wolf, 2020). It is achieved through digitization, i.e., encoding analog information in digital formats (Yoo et al., 2010) that decouple information from physical mediums and devices (Lusch & Nambisan, 2015). Therefore, digital technologies allow to "liquefy and distribute resources" within a service system and enable involved actors "quickly access and utilize resources needed for service exchange" (Barrett et al., 2015).

In *smart service systems*, smart products are a key digital technology that increasingly becomes part of value-creating systems (Fig. 2.1). *Smart products* refer to physical objects with computation, data storage, localization, sensors, actuators, and networking capability that enable learning, decision-making, and dynamic adaptation to usage situations based on data received, transmitted, and/or processed (Allmendinger & Lombreglia, 2005; National Science Foundation, 2014). Smart products can be understood as boundary objects that integrate the resources and activities of actors in service systems (Beverungen et al., 2019), and, thus, enable the co-creation of *smart service* in various forms (Boukhris & Fritzsche, 2019). Hence, smart service systems connect things and people, collect and process

J. Anke, *Smart Service Innovation*, SpringerBriefs in Information Systems,
https://doi.org/10.1007/978-3-031-43770-0_2

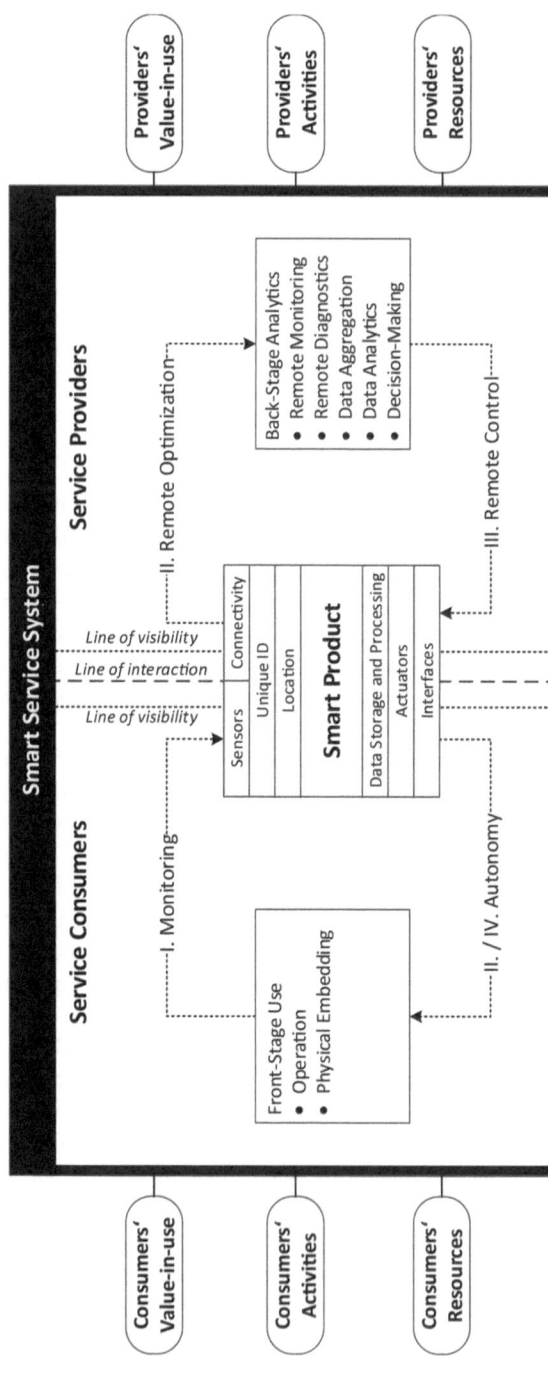

Fig. 2.1 Conceptualization of smart service systems (Beverungen et al., 2019)

data, and thereby automate and facilitate value co-creation in actor-to-actor networks (Beverungen et al., 2019; Boukhris & Fritzsche, 2019; Lim et al., 2018). This results in a wide array of potential configurations of smart service systems with different characteristics. Taxonomies can be used to support their systematic description and comparison (Brogt & Strobel, 2020).

A second research stream coming from industrial engineering conceptualized the integrated offering of goods and services as *product-service systems* (PSS) (Mont, 2002), which can enable new types of value propositions and business models (Tukker, 2004). The rising importance of information technology has extended this concept to smart PSS (Chowdhury et al., 2018; Pirola et al., 2020). A smart PSS is defined as "a PSS based on networked smart products and service systems for providing new functionalities thus leveraging on digital architectures, Internet of Things, cloud computing and analytics" (Pirola et al., 2020). Similarly, the concept of data-driven PSS (Zambetti et al., 2021) illustrates digital technology's infusion into PSS, bringing them closer to the concept of smart service systems. From an information systems perspective, IoT has been found to enable new business models and product lifecycle support in the design of PSS (Basirati et al., 2019). As a result, PSS that are enabled with IoT and other digital technologies (González Chávez et al., 2020) are particularly relevant for industrial domains, in which existing equipment, machinery, or other technical products are augmented with services or even turned into services ("servitization"), which is expected to converge with the Industry 4.0 movement (Gaiardelli et al., 2021; Kohtamäki et al., 2019).

Integrating computational capabilities into physical components has led to the concept of *cyber-physical systems* (CPS) (Wiesner et al., 2017). A CPS is "an intelligent system connecting the physical and the digital/cyber world through influence and control using sensors and actuators" (Martin et al., 2020: 14). They consist of "embedded systems, logistics and management processes, and Internet services for receiving, processing, and analyzing data from sensors, and controlling actuators connected by digital networks, and multi-modal human-machine inter-faces" (Wiesner et al., 2017). This "merging of the physical and virtual world" (Wiesner et al., 2017) allows the continuous monitoring of the environment and feedback based on data analytics.

The distinction between smart service systems, (smart) PSS, and CPS has been part of recent discussions. Beverungen et al. (2020) point out that service systems are a framework for analysis and design. In contrast, PSS refers to a marketing perspective, i.e., they are a "marketable set of products and services capable of jointly fulfilling a user's need" (Goedkoop et al., 1999). The relationship between PSS and CPS is "symbiotic" in the sense that they offer complementary perspectives: From a CPS point of view, "the physical and ICT domains are complemented with service engineering for the development of the solution" (Marilungo et al., 2017), while PSS "focuses on the bundling of tangible products and intangible services more from a business perspective" (Wiesner et al., 2017). In line with this view, this book considers PSS a smart service, which is mainly found in industrial domains. CPS provide a technological perspective on smart service systems, which helps to better understand the relationship of physical and computational aspects for observing and affecting the environment through sensors and actuators (Wiesner et al., 2017).

2.2   Service-Dominant Logic

While service science is an interdisciplinary approach that aims at designing, engineering, and managing service systems, *service-dominant logic* (SDL)—or S-D logic—originates in marketing. SDL provides a theoretical grounding of service science and hence an analysis lens for service systems, particularly the co-creation of value through interactions by multiple actors (Akaka et al., 2019; Vargo & Lusch, 2004). SDL focuses on intangible resources, relationships, and value co-creation. It thus departs from goods-dominant logic, which is centered on tangible resources, transactions, and value embedded in physical goods. SDL defines key concepts that are used throughout this book, including actor, resource, value, service, institutions, and service ecosystems (Fig. 2.2).

Actors denote any entity involved in service exchange, ranging from individual persons to firms and even nations. This view departs from traditional understanding with predefined labels such as consumers and producers, as value is understood to be co-created for each other's benefit rather than produced and consumed (Lusch & Nambisan, 2015). It also implies that value cannot be delivered by single actors.

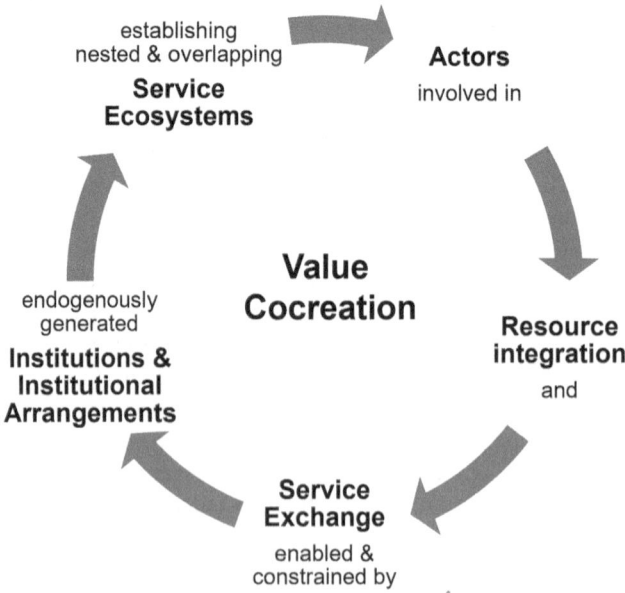

Fig. 2.2 The narrative and process of S-D logic (Vargo & Lusch, 2016)

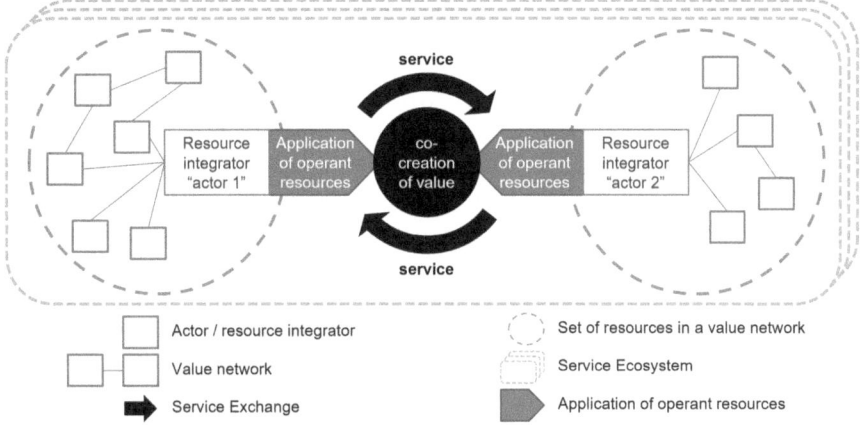

Fig. 2.3 Service exchange view of value co-creation (Ehrenthal et al., 2021)

Instead, they only can make value propositions "as an invitation to engage [..] for the cocreation of value" (Lusch & Nambisan, 2015).

Resources refer to anything that actors can draw on for support. They can be distinguished into *operand* and *operant* resources. Operand resources are acted upon and therefore have an enabling role. They are mainly static and tangible (Lusch & Nambisan, 2015), e.g., technical infrastructure. Operant resources act upon other resources to create an effect. They are typically dynamic and intangible. The most relevant type of operant resources is applied knowledge, i.e., includes human skills and capabilities. Using resources provided by other actors is called *resource integration*.

In S-D logic, *service* is the process of using one's **resources**, including specialized competencies like knowledge and skills, to benefit another **actor** or the actor itself (Lusch & Vargo, 2016; Vargo & Lusch, 2004). SDL distinctively uses the singular term "service" to denote the process character of doing something beneficial instead of the plural term "services," which would imply units of output and, hence, a goods-dominant logic (Lusch & Nambisan, 2015).

The value co-creation between two actors is achieved through the mutual application of resources from their respective value networks (Fig. 2.3). The service exchange is directed at solving problems and might involve products as a distribution mechanism. While money can be exchanged between the actors ("value-in-exchange"), the created *value* of the service is determined by the beneficiary, i.e., the customer, within the application of context ("value-in-use") (Vargo et al., 2008).

The coordination of service exchanges is supported by *institutions*, which are rules, norms, and other aids for communication. They are created by actors through institutional work and combined into more comprehensive *institutional arrangements*. Such arrangements provide the context for actor-to-actor value co-creation, e.g., projects, buyer-supplier-relations, platforms, and regulation (Barile et al., 2016). Roles describe how generic actors can engage in institutions, which can involve institutional work, i.e., the creation, maintenance, and disruption of institutions (Vargo & Lusch, 2016).

Although the S-D logic conceptualizes actors as generic, it does not mean all actors are identical (Vargo & Lusch, 2016). Instead, it refrains from assigning predesignated roles like producers and consumers to actors. Instead, it encourages to characterize actors "in terms of distinctly constituted identities associated with unique intersections of the institutional arrangements, with which they associate themselves" (Vargo & Lusch, 2016: 3). *Roles* are defined as "distinct technologically separable, value-added activities undertaken by firms or individuals" (Kambil & Short, 1994) that reflect "clusters of behaviors expected of parties in particular statuses or positions" (Knight & Harland, 2005). From an SDL perspective, a role can therefore be understood as the provision of specific resources by an actor within an institutional arrangement. While roles are usually assigned to individuals, they can also apply to organizations or other entities like groups, teams, or even networks (Story et al., 2011). Actors can have multiple roles simultaneously, and the assignment of roles to actors can change over time (Dedehayir et al., 2018; Ekman et al., 2016).

Extensions of SDL introduce the notion of *service ecosystems*, which are "relatively self-contained, self-adjusting system[s] of resource-integrating actors connected by shared institutional arrangements and mutual value creation through service exchange" (Vargo & Lusch, 2016). Such ecosystems may have multiple institutional arrangements that provide the context for service exchange. An ecosystem perspective further implies that networks of actors can be seen at various levels of aggregation as service systems and ecosystems can be nested and overlapping (Vargo & Lusch, 2016). Therefore, a service ecosystem is a service system at a higher level of aggregation; or put differently as "systems of systems" (Storbacka et al., 2016).

Disentangling the levels of aggregation, Vargo and Lusch (2017) suggest distinguishing between dyadic exchanges on a micro-level (e.g., transactions and sharing) and more complex constellations of exchanges on a meso- (e.g., networks, industries, markets) and macro-level (e.g., society) of aggregation. Taking a multi-level perspective on phenomena is at the core of the microfoundations movement in strategic management and organization theory (Felin et al., 2015; Haack et al., 2019; Storbacka et al., 2016). Microfoundations locate "the proximate causes of a phenomenon (or explanations of an outcome) at a level of analysis lower than that of the phenomenon itself" (Felin et al., 2015). That is, the actors, processes, and/or structures at the micro-level may interact or operate alone to influence phenomena at the next upper (e.g., meso- or macro-) level (Felin et al., 2015).

Grounded in S-D logic, Storbacka et al. (2016) adopt the microfoundational view to conceptualize actor engagement as a microfoundation of value co-creation in service ecosystems. They define *actor engagement* as an actor's exchange-based and non-exchange-based resource contributions in an interactive resource integration process within a service ecosystem, which is facilitated by the actor's disposition to engage (Storbacka et al., 2016; Storbacka, 2019). The framework of Storbacka et al. (2016) consists of macro-, meso-, and micro-levels (Fig. 2.4). The

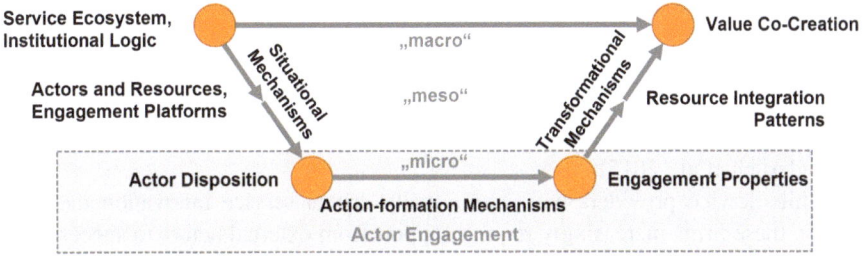

Fig. 2.4 Actor engagement as a microfoundation for value co-creation (Storbacka et al., 2016)

macro-macro relationship of their framework defines value co-creation as an outcome of service exchange within the context provided by the institutional logic of a service ecosystem (Storbacka et al., 2016, p. 3009).

Looking at the relationship between the levels, the institutional logic of a service ecosystem provides the macro-level context for the interaction of actors with their resources on engagement platforms at the meso-level. Engagement platforms are virtual or physical "environments containing artifacts, interfaces, processes and people" (Storbacka et al., 2016). They serve as intermediaries of connections between actors and facilitate but do not participate in actor engagement at the micro-level. Resource integration patterns emerge on the meso-level due to actor engagement on the micro-level. Finally, these lead to value co-creation by transforming the resource configurations of the actors in the service ecosystem (Storbacka et al., 2016).

2.3 Service Innovation in Ecosystems

Service innovation refers to the reconfiguration of resources or changes in structures and value-co-creation processes of the service system (Edvardsson & Tronvoll, 2013; Vargo et al., 2010), which lead to new practices that are useful and, hence, valuable to actors in a specific context (Edvardsson et al., 2018; Edvardsson & Tronvoll, 2013; Lusch & Nambisan, 2015). When actors (e.g., service firms) innovate, they design resource integration mechanisms, which are supposed to support other actors (e.g., customers) in integrating and acting on available resources so that they can create value in new and better ways. This view implies that service firms do not develop services (as units of output) but design and communicate new value propositions and develop and manage service systems.

The outcome of service innovation can influence multiple dimensions (Plattfaut et al., 2015), including the general service concept or value proposition, client interfaces or touchpoints, delivery system and use of technology (de Jong & Vermeulen, 2003), business partners and revenue models (den Hertog et al., 2010), as well as institutions and institutional arrangements (Edvardsson et al., 2018; Koskela-Huotari et al., 2016; Vargo & Lusch, 2016). Although SSI focuses on the use of digital technology in service systems, it usually affects multiple other dimensions at the same time as it intends to establish new and better ways of co-creating data-driven value (Beverungen et al., 2019; Djellal & Gallouj, 2018; Edvardsson et al., 2018; Maglio & Lim, 2018). Hence, the outcome of SSI can lead to a change in an actor's business model (Barrett et al., 2015; Paschou et al., 2020; Wuenderlich et al., 2015).

While service providers have traditionally driven service innovation independently, these firms increasingly require support from external actors to successfully develop new digitally enabled value propositions and corresponding resource integration mechanisms within their service ecosystems. Especially in digital transformation, service innovation no longer originates from within a single organization but evolves from "a network of actors" (Lusch & Nambisan, 2015). In other words, actors recombine elements from internal and external resources for service innovation (Beverungen et al., 2018).

Academia has just begun to investigate smart service innovation from a multi-actor perspective that goes beyond the single focal organization or the dyadic perspective of a provider and a customer actor, e.g., by identifying the roles of actors in service innovation processes (Ekman et al., 2016; Ostrom et al., 2015; Schymanietz & Jonas, 2020). Service innovation can lead to structural changes that fundamentally affect the relationship and interaction with customers (Abrell et al., 2016; Chowdhury et al., 2018; Jussen et al., 2019; Storbacka et al., 2016), e.g., by involving them as co-designers (Jonas, 2018; Martinez et al., 2010). Furthermore, the use of digital technologies in smart service systems often requires specialists in systems integration, user experience design, cloud computing, data analytics, or platform business, which are usually not available within a single organization (Djellal & Gallouj, 2018).

It is important to note that neither the involvement of actors in innovation activities nor the roles they assume are static. For example, the role of the customer can change from a supplier of ideas and creator of demands to a co-developer and tester, purchaser, and feedback provider (Dedehayir et al., 2018; Dörner et al., 2011). Similarly, consulting companies might be involved only in the early phases, while others, e.g., IoT platform providers, participate at later stages (Dedehayir et al., 2018).

The interplay of cooperating actors at each stage of the innovation process influences events in subsequent stages (Jalonen, 2012). Within this context, Edvardsson et al. (2018) propose a conceptual framework of service innovation that considers the interdependencies between the agency of actors, social structures of the service ecosystem, and different *states of the innovation process*. Their conceptualization emphasizes that service innovation must be viewed from the perspective of multiple actors and the institutional arrangements they are embedded (Edvardsson et al., 2018). Correspondingly, they distinguish between three states of the service innovation process:

- *Initiating*: formulate the intended value propositions that are attractive to other actors.

- *Realizing*: put the innovative value proposition into practice.
- *Outcoming*: market diffusion and scaling up, innovative value propositions become sustainable, and the service-providing actors can capture enough value to ensure their sustainability.

While service ecosystems are considered "emergent," actors can influence their evolution. They do so by reconfiguring institutional arrangements that guide how value is co-created within an ecosystem (Vargo et al., 2015; Vink et al., 2021). Actors that initiate or drive the innovation process may assume the role of "ecosystem orchestrator" and shape the design of such ecosystems (Lingens et al., 2021). In that view, service innovation involves a series of service exchanges between multiple actors to co-create new resources, including institutional arrangements, toward the desired value proposition for the target customer (Vargo et al., 2015). Therefore, multi-actor service innovation can be considered an ecosystem state (Chandler et al., 2019; Edvardsson et al., 2018; Polese et al., 2021).

References

Abrell, T., Pihlajamaa, M., Kanto, L., Vom Brocke, J., & Uebernickel, F. (2016). The role of users and customers in digital innovation: Insights from B2B manufacturing firms. *Information & Management, 53*, 324–335. https://doi.org/10.1016/j.im.2015.12.005

Akaka, M. A., Koskela-Huotari, K., & Vargo, S. L. (2019). Further advancing service science with service-dominant logic: Service ecosystems, institutions, and their implications for innovation. In P. P. Maglio, C. A. Kieliszewski, J. C. Spohrer, K. Lyons, L. Patrício, & Y. Sawatani (Eds.), *Handbook of service science* (pp. 641–659). Springer.

Allmendinger, G., & Lombreglia, R. (2005). Four strategies for the age of smart services. *Harvard Business Review, 83*, 131.

Barile, S., Lusch, R. F., Reynoso, J., Saviano, M., & Spohrer, J. (2016). Systems, networks, and ecosystems in service research. *Journal of Service Management, 27*, 652–674. https://doi.org/10.1108/JOSM-09-2015-0268

Barrett, M., Davidson, E., Prabhu, J., & Vargo, S. L. (2015). Service innovation in the digital age: Key contributions and future directions. *MIS Quarterly, 39*, 135–154.

Basirati, M. R., Weking, J., Hermes, S., Böhm, M., & Krcmar, H. (2019). Exploring Opportunities of IoT for Product–Service System Conceptualization and Implementation. *Asia Pacific Journal of Information Systems, 29*, 524–546. https://doi.org/10.14329/apjis.2019.29.3.524

Beverungen, D., Lüttenberg, H., & Wolf, V. (2018). Recombinant service systems engineering. *Business and Information Systems Engineering, 60*, 377–391. https://doi.org/10.1007/s12599-018-0526-4

Beverungen, D., Müller, O., Matzner, M., Mendling, J., & Vom Brocke, J. (2019). Conceptualizing smart service systems. *Electronic Markets, 29*, 7–18. https://doi.org/10.1007/s12525-017-0270-5

Beverungen, D., Kundisch, D., & Wünderlich, N. (2020). Transforming into a platform provider: Strategic options for industrial smart service providers. *Journal of Service Management, 32*, 507. https://doi.org/10.1108/JOSM-03-2020-0066

Boukhris, A., Fritzsche, A. (2019). *What is smart about services? Breaking the bond between the smart product and the service*. Research Papers.

Brogt, T., & Strobel, G. (2020). Service Systems in the era of the internet of things: A smart service system taxonomy. In *Twenty-Eighth European Conference on Information Systems*.

Chandler, J. D., Danatzis, I., Wernicke, C., Akaka, M. A., & Reynolds, D. (2019). How does innovation emerge in a service ecosystem? *Journal of Service Research, 22,* 75–89. https://doi. org/10.1177/1094670518797479

Chowdhury, S., Haftor, D., & Pashkevich, N. (2018). Smart product-service systems (smart PSS) in industrial firms: A literature review. *Procedia CIRP, 73,* 26–31. https://doi.org/10.1016/j.procir. 2018.03.333

Dedehayir, O., Mäkinen, S. J., & Roland Ortt, J. (2018). Roles during innovation ecosystem genesis: A literature review. *Technological Forecasting and Social Change, 136,* 18–29. https://doi.org/10.1016/j.techfore.2016.11.028

den Hertog, P., van der Aa, W., & de Jong, M. W. (2010). Capabilities for managing service innovation: Towards a conceptual framework. *JOSM, 21,* 490–514. https://doi.org/10.1108/ 09564231011066123

Djellal, F., & Gallouj, F. (2018). Fifteen challenges for service innovation studies. In F. Gallouj & F. Djellal (Eds.), *A research agenda for service innovation* (pp. 1–26). Edward Elgar Publishing.

Dörner, N., Gassmann, O., & Gebauer, H. (2011). Service innovation: Why is it so difficult to accomplish? *Journal of Business Strategy, 32,* 37–46. https://doi.org/10.1108/ 02756661111121983

Edvardsson, B., & Tronvoll, B. (2013). A new conceptualization of service innovation grounded in S-D logic and service systems. *International Journal of Quality & Service Sciences, 51,* 19–31.

Edvardsson, B., Tronvoll, B., & Witell, L. (2018). An ecosystem perspective on service innovation. In F. Gallouj & F. Djellal (Eds.), *A research agenda for service innovation* (pp. 85–102). Edward Elgar Publishing.

Ehrenthal, J. C. F., Gruen, T. W., & Hofstetter, J. S. (2021). Recommendations for conducting service-dominant logic research. In R. Dornberger (Ed.), *New trends in business information systems and technology* (Vol. 294, pp. 281–297). Springer International Publishing.

Ekman, P., Raggio, R. D., & Thompson, S. M. (2016). Service network value co-creation: Defining the roles of the generic actor. *Industrial Marketing Management, 56,* 51–62. https://doi.org/10. 1016/j.indmarman.2016.03.002

Felin, T., Foss, N. J., & Ployhart, R. E. (2015). The microfoundations movement in strategy and organization theory. *Academy of Management Annals, 9,* 575–632. https://doi.org/10.1080/ 19416520.2015.1007651

Gaiardelli, P., Pezzotta, G., Rondini, A., Romero, D., Jarrahi, F., Bertoni, M., Wiesner, S., Wuest, T., Larsson, T., Zaki, M., Jussen, P., Boucher, X., Bigdeli, A. Z., & Cavalieri, S. (2021). Product-service systems evolution in the era of industry 4.0. *Service Business, 15,* 177. https:// doi.org/10.1007/s11628-021-00438-9

Goedkoop, M. J., van Halen, C. J., te Riele, Harry R. M., & Rommens, P. J. M. (1999). Product service systems: Ecological and economic basics. *Report for the Dutch Ministries of Environment and Economic Affairs (No. 1999/36).* The Netherlands.

González Chávez, C. A., Despeisse, M., & Johansson, B. (2020). State-of-the-art on product-service systems and digital technologies. In Y. Kishita, M. Matsumoto, & M. Inoue (Eds.), *EcoDesign and sustainability* (pp. 71–88). Springer.

Haack, P., Sieweke, J., & Wessel, L. (2019). *Microfoundations of institutions. Research in the sociology of organizations, 65A-65B.* Emerald Publishing.

Jalonen, H. (2012). The uncertainty of innovation: a systematic review of the literature. *Journal of Management Research, 4.* https://doi.org/10.5296/jmr.v4i1.1039

Jonas, J. M. (2018). *Stakeholder integration in service innovation.* Springer Fachmedien Wiesbaden.

de Jong, J. P., & Vermeulen, P. A. (2003). Organizing successful new service development: A literature review. *Management Decision, 41,* 844–858. https://doi.org/10.1108/ 00251740310491706

Jussen, P., Kuntz, J., Senderek, R., & Moser, B. (2019). Smart service engineering. *Procedia CIRP, 83,* 384–388. https://doi.org/10.1016/j.procir.2019.04.089

Kambil, A., & Short, J. E. (1994). Electronic integration and business network redesign: A roles–linkage perspective. *Journal of Management Information Systems, 10*, 59–83. https://doi.org/10.1080/07421222.1994.11518020

Knight, L., & Harland, C. (2005). Managing supply networks. *European Management Journal, 23*, 281–292. https://doi.org/10.1016/j.emj.2005.04.006

Kohtamäki, M., Parida, V., Oghazi, P., Gebauer, H., & Baines, T. (2019). Digital servitization business models in ecosystems: A theory of the firm. *Journal of Business Research, 104*, 380–392. https://doi.org/10.1016/j.jbusres.2019.06.027

Koskela-Huotari, K., Edvardsson, B., Jonas, J. M., Sörhammar, D., & Witell, L. (2016). Innovation in service ecosystems—Breaking, making, and maintaining institutionalized rules of resource integration. *Journal of Business Research, 69*, 2964–2971. https://doi.org/10.1016/j.jbusres.2016.02.029

Lim, C., Kim, K.-H., Kim, M.-J., Heo, J.-Y., Kim, K.-J., & Maglio, P. P. (2018). From data to value: A nine-factor framework for data-based value creation in information-intensive services. *International Journal of Information Management, 39*, 121–135. https://doi.org/10.1016/j.ijinfomgt.2017.12.007

Lingens, B., Miehé, L., & Gassmann, O. (2021). The ecosystem blueprint: How firms shape the design of an ecosystem according to the surrounding conditions. *Long Range Planning, 54*, 102043. https://doi.org/10.1016/j.lrp.2020.102043

Lusch, R. F., & Nambisan, S. (2015). Service innovation: A service-dominant logic perspective. *MIS Quarterly, 39*, 155–175.

Lusch, R. F., & Vargo, S. L. (2016). Service-dominant logic: Reactions, reflections and refinements. *Marketing Theory, 6*, 281–288. https://doi.org/10.1177/1470593106066781

Maglio, P. P., & Lim, C. (2018). Innovation and smart service systems. In F. Gallouj & F. Djellal (Eds.), *A research agenda for service innovation* (pp. 103–115). Edward Elgar Publishing.

Maglio, P. P., & Spohrer, J. (2008). Fundamentals of service science. *Journal of the Academy of Marketing Science, 36*, 18–20. https://doi.org/10.1007/s11747-007-0058-9

Maglio, P. P., Vargo, S. L., Caswell, N., & Spohrer, J. (2009). The service system is the basic abstraction of service science. *Information Systems and e-Business Management, 7*, 395–406. https://doi.org/10.1007/s10257-008-0105-1

Marilungo, E., Papetti, A., Germani, M., & Peruzzini, M. (2017). From PSS to CPS design: A real industrial use case toward industry 4.0. *Procedia CIRP, 64*, 357–362. https://doi.org/10.1016/j.procir.2017.03.007

Martin, D., Kühl, N., & Maleshkova, M. (2020). Grasping the terminology: Smart services, smart service systems, and cyber-physical systems. In M. Maleshkova, N. Kühl, & P. Jussen (Eds.), *Smart service management: Design guidelines and best practices* (pp. 7–21). Springer.

Martinez, V., Bastl, M., Kingston, J., & Evans, S. (2010). Challenges in transforming manufacturing organisations into product-service providers. *Journal of Manufacturing Technology Management, 21*, 449–469. https://doi.org/10.1108/17410381011046571

Mont, O. (2002). Clarifying the concept of product–service system. *Journal of Cleaner Production, 10*, 237–245. https://doi.org/10.1016/S0959-6526(01)00039-7

Nambisan, S. (2013). Information technology and product/service innovation: A brief assessment and some suggestions for future research. *Journal of the Association for Information Systems, 14*, 215–226. https://doi.org/10.17705/1jais.00327

National Science Foundation. (2014). *Partnerships for innovation: building innovation capacity* (PFI:BIC). https://www.nsf.gov/pubs/2013/nsf13587/nsf13587.htm

Ostrom, A. L., Parasuraman, A., Bowen, D. E., Patrício, L., & Voss, C. A. (2015). Service research priorities in a rapidly changing context. *Journal of Service Research, 18*, 127–159. https://doi.org/10.1177/1094670515576315

Paschou, T., Rapaccini, M., Adrodegari, F., & Saccani, N. (2020). Digital servitization in manufacturing: A systematic literature review and research agenda. *Industrial Marketing Management, 89*, 278–292. https://doi.org/10.1016/j.indmarman.2020.02.012

Pirola, F., Boucher, X., Wiesner, S., & Pezzotta, G. (2020). Digital technologies in product-service systems: A literature review and a research agenda. *Computers in Industry, 123*, 103301. https://doi.org/10.1016/j.compind.2020.103301

Plattfaut, R., Niehaves, B., Voigt, M., Malsbender, A., Ortbach, K., & Pöppelbuß, J. (2015). Service innovation performance and information technology: An empirical analysis from the dynamic capability perspective. *International Journal of Innovation Management, 19*, 1550038. https://doi.org/10.1142/S1363919615500383

Polese, F., Payne, A., Frow, P., Sarno, D., & Nenonen, S. (2021). Emergence and phase transitions in service ecosystems. *Journal of Business Research, 127*, 25–34. https://doi.org/10.1016/j.jbusres.2020.11.067

Schymanietz, M., & Jonas, J. M. (2020). The roles of individual actors in data-driven service innovation–A dynamic capabilities perspective to explore its microfoundations. In T. Bui (Ed.), *Proceedings of the 53rd Hawaii International Conference on System Sciences*.

Sklyar, A., Kowalkowski, C., Sörhammar, D., & Tronvoll, B. (2019). Resource integration through digitalisation: A service ecosystem perspective. *Journal of Marketing Management, 35*, 974–991. https://doi.org/10.1080/0267257X.2019.1600572

Storbacka, K. (2019). Actor engagement, value creation and market innovation. *Industrial Marketing Management, 80*, 4–10. https://doi.org/10.1016/j.indmarman.2019.04.007

Storbacka, K., Brodie, R. J., Böhmann, T., Maglio, P. P., & Nenonen, S. (2016). Actor engagement as a microfoundation for value co-creation. *Journal of Business Research, 69*, 3008–3017. https://doi.org/10.1016/j.jbusres.2016.02.034

Story, V., O'Malley, L., & Hart, S. (2011). Roles, role performance, and radical innovation competences. *Industrial Marketing Management, 40*, 952–966. https://doi.org/10.1016/j.indmarman.2011.06.025

Tukker, A. (2004). Eight types of product–service system: Eight ways to sustainability? Experiences from SusProNet. *Business Strategy and the Environment, 13*, 246–260. https://doi.org/10.1002/bse.414

Vargo, S. L., & Akaka, M. A. (2012). Value Cocreation and service systems (re)formation: A service ecosystems view. *Service Science, 4*, 207–217. https://doi.org/10.1287/serv.1120.0019

Vargo, S. L., & Lusch, R. F. (2004). Evolving to a new dominant logic for marketing. *Journal of Marketing, 68*, 1–17. https://doi.org/10.1509/jmkg.68.1.1.24036

Vargo, S. L., & Lusch, R. F. (2016). Institutions and axioms: An extension and update of service-dominant logic. *Journal of the Academy of Marketing Science, 44*, 5–23. https://doi.org/10.1007/s11747-015-0456-3

Vargo, S. L., & Lusch, R. F. (2017). Service-dominant logic 2025. *International Journal of Research in Marketing, 34*, 46–67. https://doi.org/10.1016/j.ijresmar.2016.11.001

Vargo, S. L., Maglio, P. P., & Akaka, M. A. (2008). On value and value co-creation: A service systems and service logic perspective. *European Management Journal, 26*, 145–152. https://doi.org/10.1016/j.emj.2008.04.003

Vargo, S. L., Lusch, R. F., Archpru Akaka, M., & He, Y. (2010). Service-dominant logic. In N. K. Malhotra (Ed.), *Review of marketing research* (Vol. 6, pp. 125–167). Emerald Group Publishing Limited.

Vargo, S. L., Wieland, H., & Akaka, M. A. (2015). Innovation through institutionalization: A service ecosystems perspective. *Industrial Marketing Management, 44*, 63–72. https://doi.org/10.1016/j.indmarman.2014.10.008

Vink, J., Koskela-Huotari, K., Tronvoll, B., Edvardsson, B., & Wetter-Edman, K. (2021). Service ecosystem design: Propositions, process model, and future research agenda. *Journal of Service Research, 24*, 168–186. https://doi.org/10.1177/1094670520952537

Wiesner, S., Marilungo, E., & Thoben, K. D. (2017). Cyber-physical product-service systems–Challenges for requirements engineering. *International Journal of Automotive Technology, 11*, 17–28. https://doi.org/10.20965/ijat.2017.p0017

Wolf, V. (2020). Understanding smart service systems transformation–A socio-technical perspective. In *Twenty-Eighth European Conference on Information Systems*.

Wuenderlich, N. V., Heinonen, K., Ostrom, A. L., Patricio, L., Sousa, R., Voss, C., & Lemmink, J. G. (2015). "Futurizing" smart service: Implications for service researchers and managers. *Journal of Services Marketing, 29*, 442–447. https://doi.org/10.1108/JSM-01-2015-0040

Yoo, Y., Henfridsson, O., & Lyytinen, K. (2010). The new organizing logic of digital innovation: An agenda for information systems research. *Information Systems Research, 21*, 724–735. https://doi.org/10.1287/isre.1100.0322

Zambetti, M., Adrodegari, F., Pezzotta, G., Pinto, R., Rapaccini, M., & Barbieri, C. (2021). From data to value: Conceptualising data-driven product service system. *Production Planning & Control, 1–17*, 207. https://doi.org/10.1080/09537287.2021.1903113

Chapter 3
Current Approaches to the Development of Service Systems

3.1 Value Proposition Design and Business Model Innovation

Developing a value proposition attractive to the customer is at the core of service innovation. Digital technologies impact how actors create and capture value. New value propositions can yield such potentials in service innovation; hence "business model innovation can be understood as value-proposition design" (Maglio & Spohrer, 2013: 667). A well-known technique for developing value propositions is the Value Proposition Canvas (Osterwalder, 2014), which relates customer problems and needs to potential elements of new services or products. The Value Proposition Canvas has been successfully utilized for smart service business model development (Neuhüttler et al., 2018). It also serves as the foundation for methods that support the development of value propositions in smart services, e.g., the "Smart Service Canvas" (Pöppelbuß & Durst, 2019) and the "VdiP-developer" framework (Genennig et al., 2018).

Value propositions are central components of *business models* (BM), which describe "the value logic of an organization in terms of how it creates and captures customer value and can be concisely represented by an interrelated set of elements that address the customer, value proposition, organizational architecture and economics dimensions" (Fielt, 2013: 96). This definition highlights that business models include considerations of a firm-level or network-level organization as well as economic aspects for all involved actors. The basic elements of a business model and their relationships, according to Gassmann et al. (2014), are depicted in Fig. 3.1. The target customer group ("Who") is at the center and connected to the offer ("What"), the value creation resources and their orchestration ("How"), and a revenue model for value capture ("Value").

Business model innovation (BMI) aims to identify a viable combination of these elements. An analysis of existing business models has shown that many business model innovations result from recombining, modifying, or transferring existing

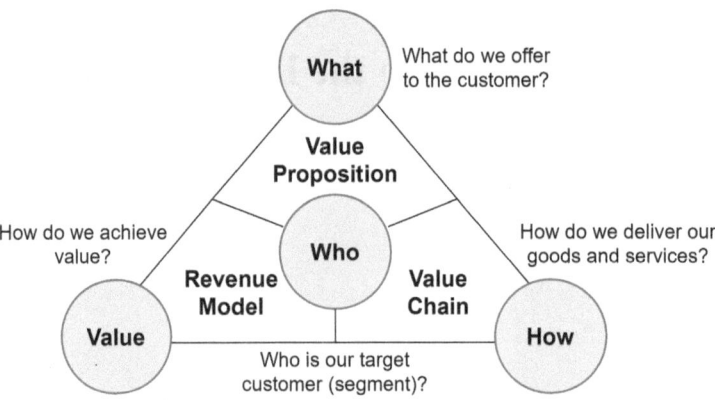

Fig. 3.1 Basic elements of a business model (Gassmann et al., 2014)

business model concepts (Gassmann et al., 2014). This finding helps to create design knowledge on business models, e.g., in the form of business model patterns. For example, the St. Gallen Business Model Navigator (Gassmann et al., 2014) supports ideation for BMI through 55 patterns, which include well-known examples such as "freemium," "pay-per-use," and "auction."

As smart services fundamentally rely on data-driven value co-creation, *data-driven business models* (DDBM) are particularly relevant (Bulger et al., 2014). Hartmann et al. (2014) define DDBM as "a business model that relies on data as a key resource." Regarding the level of data usage, there is a spectrum of business model patterns. Some use little data, while others enrich all aspects of business models with data analysis (Schüritz & Satzger, 2016). The relation between the capabilities of CPS and suitable business model patterns for smart services can be illustrated in the domain of connected cars: 16 out of the 55 patterns in the St. Gallen Business Model Navigator were identified as applicable, including "Leveraging Customer Data" and "Two-Sided Market" (Mikusz et al., 2015) for services like roadside assistance or usage-based insurance (Husnjak et al., 2015). Similarly, Turber et al. (2014) propose IoT-based business models, which highlight the relevance of data in business models and an ecosystem perspective in which multiple actors collaborate.

Service research also discusses business models (Bouwman & Fielt, 2008; Fielt, 2012; Wieland et al., 2017). They contribute to the formation of institutions, as they enable and constrain value co-creation between actors in an ecosystem (Wieland et al., 2017). Because of their characteristics, service business model representations differ from traditional business models (Ojasalo & Ojasalo, 2015). A service-specific representation is the Service Business Model Canvas (SBMC) (Zolnowski, 2015), shown in Fig. 3.2. It is based on the well-known Business Model Canvas (BMC) by Osterwalder and Pigneur (2010) but highlights the integration of different actors within service business models and, thus, allows focusing on the co-creation in the business logic. The SMBC focuses on the contribution to and benefit of each actor.

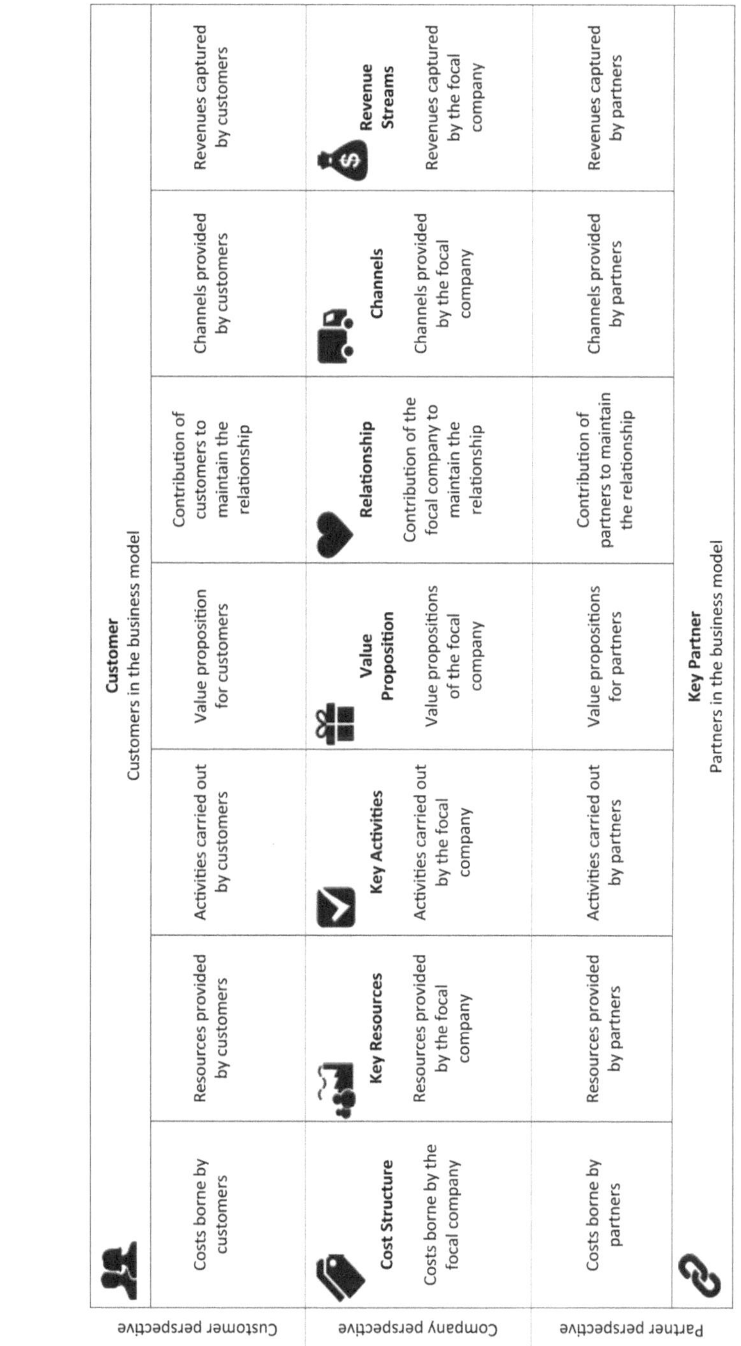

Fig. 3.2 Service Business Model Canvas (Zolnowski, 2015)

This logic is applied in seven dimensions of the original BMC, i.e., value proposition, relationship, channels, revenue streams, key resources, key activities, and cost structure. The dimensions of the customer segment and key partners are extended as separate perspectives for these actors (Zolnowski, 2015).

The information systems discipline can contribute to designing business models as strategic objects through modeling, designing artifacts, and computer-aided decision support (Osterwalder & Pigneur, 2013). For example, the emerging category of *business model design tools* (BMDT) indicates the growing software support for the definition and assessment of business models (Ebel et al., 2016; Szopinski et al., 2019), which allows for experimentation and thus facilitates business model innovation (Chesbrough, 2010).

3.2   Design Dimensions and Development Methods

Services, in general, are described along their traditional *design dimensions* of resources, process, and value (Fig. 3.3). *Resources* refer to a human or technical capacity, which is required to perform a desired change of state in the external factor, i.e., the customer itself or a customer-controlled object. Resources may include assets, technology, competencies, people, and infrastructure. *Process* describes the steps that the provider and the customer perform to create the desired service, i.e., value co-creation. The *outcome* refers to the achieved state of the external factor resulting from the process, which is valuable to the customer. Some authors include the "market" dimension, which refers to the potentially reachable customers for the service at hand, and is therefore particularly relevant for business cases and competitive analysis (Leimeister, 2020).

Bullinger et al. (2003) define outcome, process, and structure as service design dimensions that need to be described using a product model, process model, and resource concept. For the design of service systems, these dimensions can act as a high-level framework for organizing the work products created in an engineering process. Additionally, conceptual models for services rely on these design dimensions (Becker et al., 2010).

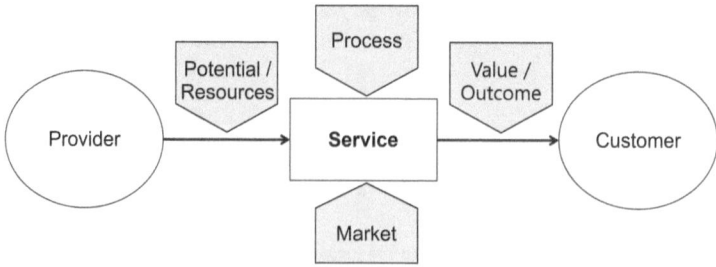

Fig. 3.3 Basic design dimensions of services (Leimeister, 2020)

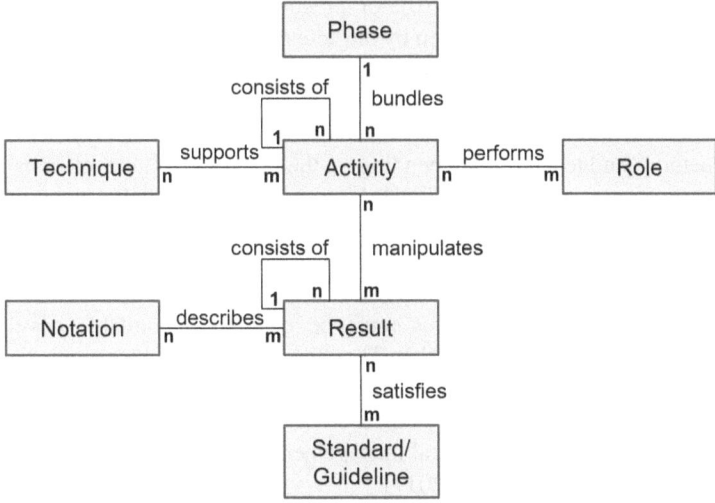

Fig. 3.4 Generic meta-model for software lifecycles (Kneuper, 2018)

To systematically develop complex systems from the initial idea for a value proposition to a production-ready system, collaborative work can be guided by *methods*. They "cover the software development process and its contained activities, but also the artifacts that are to be produced, the tasks that need to be performed to achieve the development goals, the roles in an organization that participates in the development, the tools, techniques and utilities that are employed, as well as relationships between these concepts" (Engels & Sauer, 2010: 411).

Method engineering (ME) is a discipline dealing with the systematic design, construction, and adaptation of methods for developing information systems (Brinkkemper, 1996: 276) and was later adopted for software engineering. As ME requires the consideration of methods on a meta-level, it provides the terminological basis of key concepts such as method, technique, tool, and notation (Brinkkemper, 1996). These concepts are applied for describing, analyzing, and improving (software) development processes. For that, meta-models for engineering processes help to establish the links between the sequencing of activities as a process, the roles of the persons responsible for conducting these activities, and the techniques that support the performance of activities (Engels & Sauer, 2010). Standards, guidelines, and notations describe the structure of a particular artifact and therefore facilitate the documentation of results, i.e., work products. A generic meta-model for the software lifecycle is depicted in Fig. 3.4.

It has been acknowledged that there is no "one-size-fits-all" approach to development processes, as the specifics of projects and organizations are never fully considered in standardized methods. *Situational Method Engineering* (SME) (Henderson-Sellers & Ralyté, 2010) suggests that the method for a specific (software) development endeavor should be created from existing—more or less formalized—parts which are called method fragments, method chunks

(Henderson-Sellers & Ralyté, 2010), or practices (Jacobson et al., 2007). The selection and composition are driven by the actual context, described by "situational factors," such as team size, application size, requirements stability, organizational culture, business risks, and legal aspects (Clarke & O'Connor, 2012).

As Alt (2019) points out, the transformation of organizations requires different sets of methods and techniques depending on the transformation level, consisting of software, processes, and value. With the focus on value in digital transformation, techniques like the BMC and methods like business model innovation are applied to guide transformation projects (Alt, 2019). With smart service systems consisting of a technical software-intensive system, a service process, and often an innovative business model, these perspectives must be covered by suitable development approaches (Pakkala & Spohrer, 2019). Therefore, methods from various disciplines may be applied in SSI, including service engineering, PSS engineering, software engineering, business model innovation, systems engineering, user-centered design, innovation management, and general management (Abramovici et al., 2015; Hagen et al., 2018a; Kuhlenkötter et al., 2017).

Selecting and combining suitable parts from existing methods can serve as a basis for organizing SSI projects. Vink et al. (2021) call for the development of practical methods and approaches for collaborative service design in ecosystems. It shows both the growing awareness of such setups and the lack of methods to exploit their potential. From an SDL perspective, reference models, methods, and frameworks are institutional arrangements, providing norms, rules, and practices that enable and constrain actors' work (Iden et al., 2020). Projects facilitate resource integration and service exchanges between actors (Vargo & Clavier, 2015), so they represent the meso-level in the multi-level SSI framework.

3.3　Service Engineering and Service Systems Engineering

Developing a service system that fulfills the envisioned value proposition is complex. *Service engineering* (SE[1]) is "a technical discipline concerned with the systematic development and design of services using suitable procedures, methods, and tools" (Bullinger et al., 2003). It aims to adapt methods for product engineering to make them useable for service development (Böhmann et al., 2014) and follow a rather traditional linear approach (Beverungen et al., 2018). However, these procedural models are poorly established in practice (Hagen et al., 2018b).

In *PSS engineering*, a large body of knowledge has emerged (Cavalieri & Pezzotta, 2012). As PSS and smart service systems share the characteristics of high complexity in both the engineering process and the resulting system, existing

---

[1]SE is often used as abbreviation for software engineering. As both software engineering and service engineering are relevant in this book, it is important to note that software engineering will always be written out while SE always stands for service engineering.

methods for PSS engineering may inform smart service innovation. Studies regarding the suitability of PSS engineering methods for smart PSS have found that methods and frameworks are applicable but need to be enhanced to support customer integration and specifics of digital technologies better (Hagen et al., 2018a; Pirola et al., 2020).

In order to address the specific characteristics and potentials of smart services, methods need to consider the role of data as a resource and the use of digital technologies in service systems (Demirkan et al., 2015; Herterich et al., 2016). This deficit has led to a call for the development of new service engineering methods, which also apply S-D logic, i.e., consider multi-actor value co-creation in service systems (Peters et al., 2016). Although improvement and adaption of existing methods for the digital age are ongoing, they do not sufficiently address smart services' increased complexity and agility (Marx et al., 2020).

A recent study assessed 36 SE methods toward their suitability for smart services from a service, product, data, and software perspective and five phases of a development process (Marx et al., 2020). It found that only 12 methods consider smart services, while most methods focus on PSS. Regarding comprehensiveness, the service perspective is addressed by all methods, while software and data are only considered in 6 and 11 cases, respectively. The requirements and design phases are covered the most in the development process, while idea generation, implementation, and delivery received far less attention (Marx et al., 2020). Only a single method (Freitag & Wiesner, 2018) covers all development phases but focuses on the service perspective. Another method partially covers all perspectives but is limited to the design phase (Verdugo Cedeño et al., 2018). Interestingly, both methods build upon Product Lifecycle Management (PLM) (Terzi et al., 2010), which provides a comprehensive foundation for designing and managing services around smart products (Kiritsis, 2011).

Service systems engineering (SSE) is an emerging discipline that takes service systems as the basic unit of analysis and design and thus adopts a systemic perspective on service innovation. It addresses the engineering of (1) service architectures, (2) service systems interactions, and (3) resource mobilization and aims to provide models, methods, and artifacts to support these activities (Böhmann et al., 2014; Grotherr et al., 2018). Figure 3.5 depicts the main elements of service systems targeted by SSE and examples from smart service systems. While BMI helps to develop novel value propositions, SSE aims to engineer the service system that enables them.

In the context of SSE, the potential of CPS regarding data acquisition and automation is identified as an enabler for service innovation (Böhmann et al., 2014) that leads to smart service systems. Several approaches have recently been proposed for SSE in the academic literature, e.g.:

- *Engineering of digitally enabled service systems* combines the existing methods with a new approach for liquifying, unbundling, and re-bundling resources (Höckmayr & Roth, 2017).

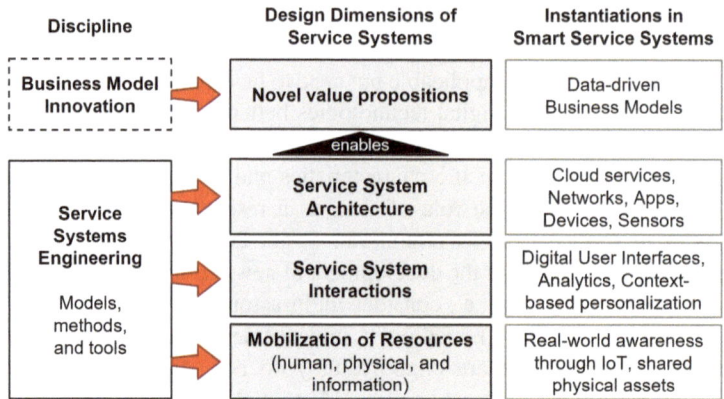

Discipline	Design Dimensions of Service Systems	Instantiations in Smart Service Systems
Business Model Innovation	Novel value propositions	Data-driven Business Models

enables

Service Systems Engineering Models, methods, and tools	Service System Architecture	Cloud services, Networks, Apps, Devices, Sensors
	Service System Interactions	Digital User Interfaces, Analytics, Context-based personalization
	Mobilization of Resources (human, physical, and information)	Real-world awareness through IoT, shared physical assets

Fig. 3.5 Service systems engineering (SSE) in context (based on Böhmann et al., 2014)

- *Recombinant Service Engineering* (Beverungen et al., 2018) aims to create a class of methods for service systems through association, dissociation, and recombination of existing resources.
- *Multi-level design framework for service systems* (Grotherr et al., 2018) guides the process of iterative design and validation of design decisions through real-world interventions.
- *Smart Service Engineering* (Jussen et al., 2019; Moser & Faulhaber, 2020) integrates business model development and prototyping in ecosystems into a lightweight agile process.
- *DIN SPEC 33453 "Development of Digital Service Systems"* (2019) consists of design dimensions, phases, activities, and methods to support the conduct of activities (Fig. 3.6).

Further SSE approaches consider specific aspects of smart service systems, e.g., data-driven value-creation (Lim et al., 2018), platforms (Adali et al., 2021), multi-actor value networks (Patrício et al., 2018; Reinhold et al., 2021), ecosystems (Immonen et al., 2016), and service architecture (Halstenberg et al., 2019). Another group of methods addresses the specifics of smart service for manufacturing and industrial equipment (Freitag & Hämmerle, 2020).

Some development approaches use product models to document the current state of the developed system concept and show the interdependencies of system elements, particularly in methods that follow the model-based systems engineering (MBSE) approach (Halstenberg et al., 2019). There is a variety of modeling approaches, which can be differentiated into general modeling languages and domain-specific languages: *Modeling languages* allow the description of complex systems and value creation structures in various domains, e.g., e3-Value (Gordijn, 2004), Business Process Model and Notation (BPMN), the System Modeling Language (SysML), the Unified Modeling Language (UML), and the Lifecycle Modeling Language (LML). As they are targeted at describing different aspects of a system (Halstenberg et al., 2019), they are often used in parallel.

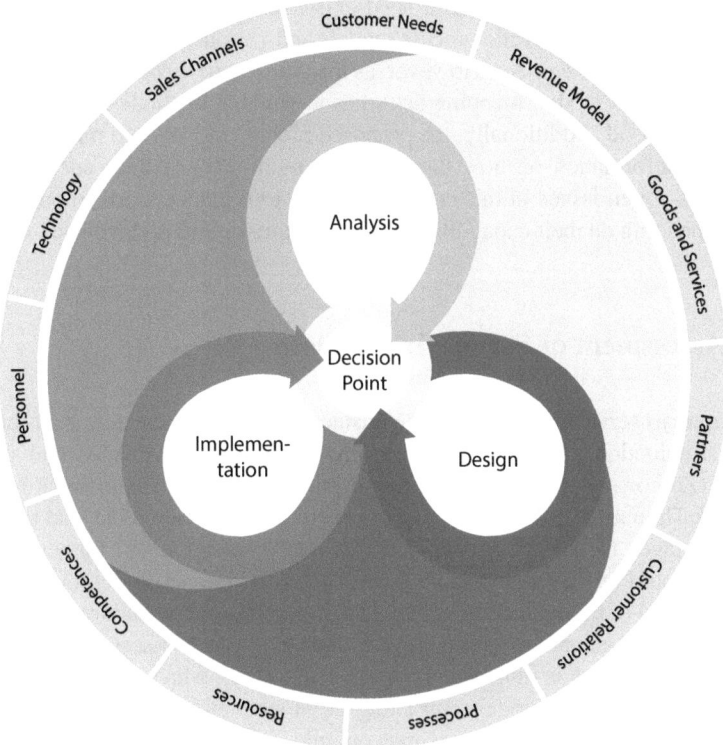

Fig. 3.6 DIN SPEC 33453 Reference process and design dimensions for digital service systems (Beverungen et al., 2021)

More recently, *domain-specific languages* (DSL) for smart service have been suggested (Huber et al., 2019; Lessard et al., 2020; Lüttenberg, 2020; Strobel, 2021). They capture the specifics of smart service systems through a meta-model, often expressed as UML class diagrams. This meta-model provides the abstract syntax, which may be augmented through a concrete syntax (notation) that visually represents the defined modeling elements.

The plethora of methods in this space illustrates the ongoing effort of researchers to understand the specifics of smart service systems and address them in suitable development approaches. Notwithstanding this variety, most methods and process models highlight the importance of agility, i.e., they follow the principles of the "Agile Manifesto" (Beck et al., 2001). It contains a set of values and principles calling for the organization of development efforts in a highly iterative way with intensive customer involvement. Adopting agile practices helps to adapt to dynamics in the environment (Kuhrmann et al., 2021; Paez et al., 2020; Paluch et al., 2020) and thus addresses the complexity and uncertainty inherent to SSI (Ramirez Hernandez & Kreye, 2020; Sjödin et al., 2020a).

Overall, a widely acknowledged need exists for better guidance in engineering (smart) service systems. Agile process models and various methods directly address the specifics of smart services. However, as many methods were developed without a particular process model, mapping activities to suitable methods and techniques is poorly understood. Additionally, the proposed process models and methods provide barely any information on how they work in multi-actor settings such as service ecosystems. Open issues in this context are how to organize work among multiple actors depending on their capabilities and how actors should perform their activities.

3.4 Assessment of Service Innovations

Offering smart services and data-driven business models may create various benefits, e.g., cost reduction, increased revenues, improved customer loyalty, and strategic benefits (Zolnowski et al., 2016). However, not all these expectations are fulfilled (Hagen & Thomas, 2019). Successful smart service innovation must lead to sustainable advantages for all actors involved in value co-creation. To this end, service concepts should be assessed regarding their potential impact. Assessment methods require a model of the evaluation target, a set of criteria, and procedures for gathering and combining evaluation-related aspects into an overall assessment result. The complexity of the task is illustrated by Kim et al. (2016), who propose an evaluation scheme for PSS system models consisting of 94 evaluation criteria that cover both customer and provider perspectives in economic, environmental, and social dimensions along the complete lifecycle. This list serves as a repository for users to select suitable criteria depending on evaluation targets.

Business models are frequently used to develop and refine the business logic of a service idea, thus impacting the service's economic value. Therefore, they lend themselves as a vehicle for assessment, which can guide both the design of the service and the business model itself. Tesch et al. (2017) argue that assessments of service business models should be performed in early lifecycle phases, e.g., to decide which service idea should be pursued further and justify funding. Determining costs and benefits can influence business model design decisions (Turetken et al., 2019). As business models are qualitative (Zott et al., 2011), they need to be augmented with additional information to enable quantitative assessments. Meertens et al. (2014) propose a method for assessing business model alternatives through derived business cases. Other methods guide the concretization of cost and benefit (Gilsing et al., 2020) or evaluate digitalization opportunities through the financial assessment of new business models (Linde et al., 2021).

Research on service assessment methods is still nascent. For example, PSS engineering methods call for a "business analysis" to determine the financial impact, but only a few PSS design models contain concrete activities for economic analysis (Lin & Hsieh, 2011; Marques et al., 2016). Pirola et al. (2020) identify the assessment of PSS concepts as one of the main but least addressed research streams for smart PSS. Their study focuses on tools that allow PSS concepts' quantitative and

qualitative assessments to foresee their economic and business value. The authors emphasize the relevance of PSS assessment for managing risk and uncertainty using economic models, e.g., to predict costs at an early design stage. They acknowledge that the created value of smart PSS is distributed among multiple actors, which makes assessment using economic models difficult (Pirola et al., 2020). One of the most recent proposals for economic assessment uses a PSS model, which is iteratively developed in a software tool (Medini et al., 2021). Based on a simulation, the tool calculates the cost and revenue of the modeled PSS along its lifecycle for both the customer and the provider.

It can be concluded that the assessment of service ideas and business models is an under-researched area. While the importance of such assessments is recognized, the knowledge of methods and their integration into the design process is sparse and fragmented. In line with agile principles, several authors suggest that such assessments should be performed early and repeatedly to create insights to support design decisions. Assessments should therefore be part of an iterative design process as proposed in recent frameworks for risk-oriented smart PSS engineering (Coba et al., 2020) and value-driven business model design (Sjödin et al., 2020b).

References

DIN SPEC 33453. (2019). *DIN SPEC 33453 Entwicklung digitaler Dienstleistungssysteme*. DIN.

Abramovici, M., Göbel, J. C., & Neges, M. (2015). Smart engineering as enabler for the 4th industrial revolution. In M. Fathi (Ed.), *Integrated systems: Innovations and applications* (pp. 163–170). Springer International Publishing.

Adali, O. E., Ozkan, B., Turetken, O., & Grefen, P. (2021). Identification of service platform requirements from value propositions: A service systems engineering method. In L. M. Camarinha-Matos, X. Boucher, & H. Afsarmanesh (Eds.), *Smart and sustainable collaborative networks 4.0* (Vol. 629, pp. 311–322). Springer International Publishing.

Alt, R. (2019). Electronic markets on digital transformation methodologies. *Electronic Markets, 29*, 307–313. https://doi.org/10.1007/s12525-019-00370-x

Beck K, Beedle M, van Bennekum A, Cockburn A, Cunningham W, Fowler M, Grenning J, Highsmith J, Hunt A, Jeffries R, Kern J, Marick B (2001) Manifesto for agile software development. Accessed Dec 18, 2021, from https://agilemanifesto.org/

Becker, J., Beverungen, D. F., & Knackstedt, R. (2010). The challenge of conceptual modeling for product–service systems: Status-quo and perspectives for reference models and modeling languages. *Information Systems and e-Business Management, 8*, 33–66. https://doi.org/10.1007/s10257-008-0108-y

Beverungen, D., Lüttenberg, H., & Wolf, V. (2018). Recombinant service systems engineering. *Business and Information Systems Engineering, 60*, 377–391. https://doi.org/10.1007/s12599-018-0526-4

Beverungen, D., Wolf, V., Bartelheimer, C., & Franke, A. (2021). Digitale Transformation von Dienstleistungssystemen–Beidhändige Innovationen für vernetzte Wertschöpfungsszenarien. In D. Beverungen, J. H. Schumann, V. Stich, & G. Strina (Eds.), *Dienstleistungsinnovationen durch Digitalisierung* (pp. 3–41). Springer.

Böhmann, T., Leimeister, J. M., & Möslein, K. (2014). Service systems engineering. *Business and Information Systems Engineering, 6*, 73–79. https://doi.org/10.1007/s12599-014-0314-8

Bouwman, H., & Fielt, E. (2008). Service innovation and business models. In H. Bouwman & T. Haaker (Eds.), *Mobile service innovation and business models* (pp. 9–30). Springer.

Brinkkemper, S. (1996). Method engineering: Engineering of information systems development methods and tools. *Information and Software Technology, 38*, 275–280. https://doi.org/10.1016/0950-5849(95)01059-9

Bulger, M., Taylor, G., & Schroeder, R. (2014) *Data-driven business models: Challenges and opportunities of big data.*

Bullinger, H.-J., Fähnrich, K.-P., & Meiren, T. (2003). Service engineering—Methodical development of new service products. *International Journal of Production Economics, 85*, 275–287. https://doi.org/10.1016/S0925-5273(03)00116-6

Cavalieri, S., & Pezzotta, G. (2012). Product–service systems engineering: State of the art and research challenges. *Computers in Industry, 63*, 278–288. https://doi.org/10.1016/j.compind.2012.02.006

Chesbrough, H. (2010). Business model innovation: Opportunities and barriers. *Long Range Planning, 43*, 354–363. https://doi.org/10.1016/j.lrp.2009.07.010

Clarke, P., & O'Connor, R. V. (2012). The situational factors that affect the software development process: Towards a comprehensive reference framework. *Information and Software Technology, 54*, 433–447. https://doi.org/10.1016/j.infsof.2011.12.003

Coba, C. M., Boucher, X., Gonzalez-Feliu, J., Vuillaume, F., & Gay, A. (2020). Towards a risk-oriented smart PSS engineering framework. *Procedia CIRP, 93*, 753–758. https://doi.org/10.1016/j.procir.2020.03.054

Demirkan, H., Bess, C., Spohrer, J., Rayes, A., Allen, D., & Moghaddam, Y. (2015). Innovations with smart service systems: Analytics, big data, cognitive assistance, and the internet of everything. *Communications of the Association for Information Systems, 37*.

Ebel, P., Bretschneider, U., & Leimeister, J. M. (2016). Leveraging virtual business model innovation: A framework for designing business model development tools. *Information Systems Journal, 26*, 519–550. https://doi.org/10.1111/isj.12103

Engels, G., & Sauer, S. (2010). A meta-method for defining software engineering methods. In G. Engels, C. Lewerentz, W. Schäfer, A. Schürr, & B. Westfechtel (Eds.), *Graph transformations and model-driven engineering* (Vol. 5765, pp. 411–440). Springer Nature.

Fielt, E. (2012). A 'service logic' rationale for business model innovation. In *EURAM Annual Conference*.

Fielt, E. (2013). Conceptualising business models: Definitions, frameworks and classifications. *Journal of Business Models, 1*, 85–105.

Freitag, M., & Hämmerle, O. (2020). Agile guideline for development of smart services in manufacturing enterprises with support of artificial intelligence. In B. Lalic, V. Majstorovic, U. Marjanovic, G. von Cieminski, & D. Romero (Eds.), *Advances in production management systems: The path to digital transformation and innovation of production management systems: IFIP WG 5. 7 International Conference, APMS 2020, Novi Sad, Serbia, Proceedings* (Vol. 591, pp. 645–652). Springer.

Freitag, M., & Wiesner, S. (2018). Smart service lifecycle management: A framework and use case. In I. Moon, G. M. Lee, J. Park, D. Kiritsis, & G. von Cieminski (Eds.), *Advances in Production Management Systems. Smart Manufacturing for Industry 4.0: IFIP WG 5.7 International Conference, APMS 2018, Seoul, Korea, Proceedings, Part II* (Vol. 536, pp. 97–104). Springer International Publishing.

Gassmann, O., Frankenberger, K., & Csik, M. (2014). Revolutionizing the business model. In O. Gassmann & F. Schweitzer (Eds.), *Management of the Fuzzy Front end of innovation* (pp. 89–97). Springer International Publishing.

Genennig, S. M., Roth, A., Jonas, J. M., & Moslein, K. M. (2018). Value propositions in service systems enabled by digital technology: A field based design science approach. *SMR, 2*, 6–21. https://doi.org/10.15358/2511-8676-2018-4-6

Gilsing, R., Turetken, O., Ozkan, B., Slaats, F., Adali, O. E., Wilbik, A., Berkers, F., & Grefen, P. (2020). A method to guide the concretization of costs and benefits in service-dominant

business models. In L. M. Camarinha-Matos, H. Afsarmanesh, & A. Ortiz (Eds.), *Boosting collaborative networks 4.0* (Vol. 598, pp. 61–70). Springer International Publishing.

Gordijn, J. (2004). E-business value modelling using the e3-value ontology. In *Value creation from E-business models* (pp. 98–127). Elsevier.

Grotherr, C., Semmann, M., & Böhmann, T. (2018). Using microfoundations of value co-creation to guide service systems design–A multilevel design framework. In *Thirty Ninth International Conference on Information Systems*.

Hagen, S., & Thomas, O. (2019). Expectations vs. reality–benefits of smart services in the field of tension between industry and science. In *Proceedings of Internationale Tagung Wirtschaftsinformatik*.

Hagen, S., Kammler, F., & Thomas, O. (2018a). Adapting product-service system methods for the digital era: Requirements for smart PSS engineering. In S. Hankammer, K. Nielsen, F. T. Piller, G. Schuh, & N. Wang (Eds.), *Customization 4.0* (Vol. 97, pp. 87–99). Springer International Publishing.

Hagen, S., Jannaber, S., & Thomas, O. (2018b). Closing the gap between research and practice—A study on the usage of service engineering development methods in German enterprises. In G. Satzger, L. Patrício, M. Zaki, N. Kühl, & P. Hottum (Eds.), *Exploring Service Science: 9th International Conference, IESS 2018, Karlsruhe, Germany, Proceedings* (Vol. 331, pp. 59–71). Springer International Publishing.

Halstenberg, F. A., Lindow, K., & Stark, R. (2019). Leveraging circular economy through a methodology for smart service systems engineering. *Sustainability, 11*, 3517. https://doi.org/10.3390/su11133517

Hartmann, P. M., Zaki, M., Feldmann, N., & Neely, A. (2014). Big data for big business?: A taxonomy of data-driven business models used by start-up firms. A taxonomy of data-driven business models used by start-up firms. *Social Science Research Network*.

Henderson-Sellers, B., & Ralyté, J. (2010). Situational method engineering: State-of-the-art review. *Journal of Universal Computer Science, 16*, 424–478.

Herterich, M., Eck, A., & Uebernickel, F. (2016). Exploring how digitized products enable industrial service innovation–an affordance perspective. In *Proceedings of the 24th European Conference on Information Systems*.

Höckmayr, B., & Roth, A. (2017). Design of a Method for service systems engineering in the digital age. In Y. J. Kim, R. Agarwal, & J. K. Lee (Eds.), *Proceedings of the International Conference on Information Systems–Transforming Society with Digital Innovation, ICIS 2017, Seoul, South Korea*. Association for Information Systems.

Huber, R. X. R., Püschel, L. C., & Röglinger, M. (2019). Capturing smart service systems: Development of a domain-specific modelling language. *Information Systems Journal, 29*, 1207–1255. https://doi.org/10.1111/isj.12269

Husnjak, S., Peraković, D., Forenbacher, I., & Mumdziev, M. (2015). Telematics system in usage based motor insurance. *Procedia Engineering, 100*, 816–825. https://doi.org/10.1016/j.proeng.2015.01.436

Iden, J., Eikebrokk, T. R., & Marrone, M. (2020). Process reference frameworks as institutional arrangements for digital service innovation. *International Journal of Information Management, 54*, 102150. https://doi.org/10.1016/j.ijinfomgt.2020.102150

Immonen, A., Ovaska, E., Kalaoja, J., & Pakkala, D. (2016). A service requirements engineering method for a digital service ecosystem. *Service Oriented Computing and Applications, 10*, 151–172. https://doi.org/10.1007/s11761-015-0175-0

Jacobson, I., Ng, P. W., & Spence, I. (2007). Enough of processes–lets do practices. *Journal of Object Technology, 6*, 41. https://doi.org/10.5381/jot.2007.6.6.c5

Jussen, P., Kuntz, J., Senderek, R., & Moser, B. (2019). Smart service engineering. *Procedia CIRP, 83*, 384–388. https://doi.org/10.1016/j.procir.2019.04.089

Kim, K.-J., Lim, C.-H., Heo, J.-Y., Lee, D.-H., Hong, Y.-S., & Park, K. (2016). An evaluation scheme for product–service system models: Development of evaluation criteria and case studies. *Service Business, 10*, 507–530. https://doi.org/10.1007/s11628-015-0280-3

Kiritsis, D. (2011). Closed-loop PLM for intelligent products in the era of the internet of things. *Computer-Aided Design, 43*, 479–501. https://doi.org/10.1016/j.cad.2010.03.002

Kneuper, R. (2018). *Software processes and life cycle models: An introduction to modelling, using and managing agile, plan-driven and hybrid processes.* Springer International Publishing.

Kuhlenkötter, B., Wilkens, U., Bender, B., Abramovici, M., Süße, T., Göbel, J., Herzog, M., Hypki, A., & Lenkenhoff, K. (2017). New perspectives for generating smart PSS solutions–Life cycle, methodologies and transformation. *Procedia CIRP, 64*, 217–222. https://doi.org/10.1016/j.procir.2017.03.036

Kuhrmann, M., Tell, P., Hebig, R., Klunder, J. A.-C., Munch, J., Linssen, O., Pfahl, D., Felderer, M., Prause, C., Macdonell, S., Nakatumba-Nabende, J., Raffo, D., Beecham, S., Tuzun, E., Lopez, G., Paez, N., Fontdevila, D., Licorish, S., Kupper, S., Ruhe, G., Knauss, E., Ozcan-Top, O., Clarke, P., Mc Caffery, F. H., Genero, M., Vizcaino, A., Piattini, M., Kalinowski, M., Conte, T., Prikladnicki, R., Krusche, S., Coskuncay, A., Scott, E., Calefato, F., Pimonova, S., Pfeiffer, R.-H., Pagh Schultz, U., Heldal, R., Fazal-Baqaie, M., Anslow, C., Nayebi, M., Schneider, K., Sauer, S., Winkler, D., Biffl, S., Bastarrica, C., & Richardson, I. (2021). What makes agile software development agile. *IIEEE Trans. Software Eng.:1., 48*, 3523. https://doi.org/10.1109/TSE.2021.3099532

Leimeister, J. M. (2020). *Dienstleistungsengineering und -management: Data-driven Service Innovation* (2nd ed.). Lehrbuch.

Lessard, L., Amyot, D., Aswad, O., & Moutham, A. (2020). Expanding the nature and scope of requirements for service systems through service-dominant logic: The case of a telemonitoring service. *Requirements Engineering, 25*, 273–293. https://doi.org/10.1007/s00766-019-00322-z

Lim, C., Kim, K.-H., Kim, M.-J., Heo, J.-Y., Kim, K.-J., & Maglio, P. P. (2018). From data to value: A nine-factor framework for data-based value creation in information-intensive services. *International Journal of Information Management, 39*, 121–135. https://doi.org/10.1016/j.ijinfomgt.2017.12.007

Lin, F.-R., & Hsieh, P.-S. (2011). A SAT view on new service development. *Service Science, 3*, 141–157. https://doi.org/10.1287/serv.3.2.141

Linde, L., Sjödin, D., Parida, V., & Gebauer, H. (2021). Evaluation of digital business model opportunities. *Research-Technology Management, 64*, 43–53. https://doi.org/10.1080/08956308.2021.1842664

Lüttenberg, H. (2020). PS3–A domain-specific modeling language for platform-based smart service systems. In S. Hofmann, O. Müller, & M. Rossi (Eds.), *Designing for digital transformation. Co-creating services with citizens and industry. DESRIST 2020.: 15th* (Vol. 12388, pp. 438–450). Springer Nature.

Maglio, P. P., & Spohrer, J. (2013). A service science perspective on business model innovation. *Industrial Marketing Management, 42*, 665–670. https://doi.org/10.1016/j.indmarman.2013.05.007

Marques, C. A. N., Mendes, G. H. S., Oliveira, M. G., & Rozenfeld, H. (2016). Comparing PSS design models based on content analysis. *Procedia CIRP, 47*, 144–149. https://doi.org/10.1016/j.procir.2016.03.068

Marx, E., Pauli, T., Fielt, E., & Matzner, M. (2020). From services to smart services: Can service engineering methods get smarter as well? In *15th International Conference on Wirtschaftsinformatik.*

Medini, K., Peillon, S., Orellano, M., Wiesner, S., & Liu, A. (2021). System modelling and analysis to support economic assessment of product-service systems. *Systems, 9*, 6. https://doi.org/10.3390/systems9010006

Meertens, L. O., Starreveld, E., Iacob, M.-E., & Nieuwenhuis, B. (2014). Creating a business case from a business model. In B. Shishkov (Ed.), *Business modeling and software design: Third international symposium, BMSD 2013* (Vol. 173, pp. 46–63). Springer.

Mikusz, M., Jud, C., & Schäfer, T. (2015). Business model patterns for the connected car and the example of data orchestrator. In J. M. Fernandes, R. J. Machado, & K. Wnuk (Eds.), *Software business: 6ᵗʰ International Conference, ICSOB 2015, Braga, Portugal* (Vol. 210, pp. 167–173). Springer.

Moser, B., & Faulhaber, M. (2020). Smart service engineering. In M. Maleshkova, N. Kühl, & P. Jussen (Eds.), *Smart service management: Design guidelines and best practices* (pp. 45–61). Springer.

Neuhüttler, J., Woyke, I. C., & Ganz, W. (2018). Applying value proposition design for developing smart service business models in manufacturing firms. In L. E. Freund & W. Cellary (Eds.), *Advances in the human side of service engineering* (pp. 103–114).

Ojasalo, K., & Ojasalo, J. (2015). Adapting business model thinking to service logic: An empirical study on developing a service design tool. *The Nordic School, 309.*

Osterwalder, A. (2014). *Value proposition design: How to create products and services customers want.* Strategyzer series. John Wiley & Sons.

Osterwalder, A., & Pigneur, Y. (2010). *Business model generation: A handbook for visionaries game changers and challengers.* Wiley.

Osterwalder, A., & Pigneur, Y. (2013). Designing business models and similar strategic objects: The contribution of IS. *Journal of the Association for Information Systems, 14,* 237–244. https://doi.org/10.17705/1jais.00333

Paez, N., Fontdevila, D., & Oliveros, A. (2020). On the influence of agile in the usage of software development practices. In *2020 IEEE Congreso Bienal de Argentina (ARGENCON)* (pp. 1–7). IEEE.

Pakkala, D., & Spohrer, J. (2019). Digital service: Technological Agency in Service Systems. In T. Bui (Ed.), *Proceedings of the 52ⁿᵈ Hawaii international conference on system sciences.* Hawaii International Conference on System Sciences.

Paluch, S., Antons, D., Brettel, M., Hopp, C., Salge, T.-O., Piller, F., & Wentzel, D. (2020). Stage-gate and agile development in the digital age: Promises, perils, and boundary conditions. *Journal of Business Research, 110,* 495–501. https://doi.org/10.1016/j.jbusres.2019.01.063

Patrício, L., de Pinho, N. F., Teixeira, J. G., & Fisk, R. P. (2018). Service Design for Value Networks: Enabling value Cocreation interactions in healthcare. *Service Science, 10,* 76–97. https://doi.org/10.1287/serv.2017.0201

Peters, C., Maglio, P. P., Badinelli, R., Harmon, R. R., Maull, R., Spohrer, J. C., Tuunanen, T., Vargo, S. L., Welser, J. J., Demirkan, H., Griffith, T. L., & Moghaddam, Y. (2016). Emerging digital Frontiers for service innovation. *Communications of the Association for Information Systems, 39,* 136–149. https://doi.org/10.17705/1CAIS.03908

Pirola, F., Boucher, X., Wiesner, S., & Pezzotta, G. (2020). Digital technologies in product-service systems: A literature review and a research agenda. *Computers in Industry, 123,* 103301. https://doi.org/10.1016/j.compind.2020.103301

Pöppelbuß, J., & Durst, C. (2019). Smart service canvas–A tool for analyzing and designing smart product-service systems. *Procedia CIRP, 83,* 324–329. https://doi.org/10.1016/j.procir.2019.04.077

Ramirez Hernandez, T., & Kreye, M. E. (2020). Uncertainty profiles in engineering-service development: Exploring supplier co-creation. *Journal of Service Management., 32,* 407. https://doi.org/10.1108/JOSM-08-2019-0270

Reinhold, J., Ködding, P., Scholtysik, M., Koldewey, C., & Dumitrescu, R. (2021). Identifying value creation patterns for smart services. *Procedia CIRP, 104,* 576–581. https://doi.org/10.1016/j.procir.2021.11.097

Schüritz, R., & Satzger, G. (2016). Patterns of data-infused business model innovation. In E. Kornyshova (Ed.), *18ᵗʰ IEEE conference on business informatics: Proceedings: Paris, France. Conference Publishing Services* (pp. 133–142). IEEE Computer Society.

Sjödin, D., Parida, V., Kohtamäki, M., & Wincent, J. (2020a). An agile co-creation process for digital servitization: A micro-service innovation approach. *Journal of Business Research, 112,* 478–491. https://doi.org/10.1016/j.jbusres.2020.01.009

Sjödin, D., Parida, V., Jovanovic, M., & Visnjic, I. (2020b). Value creation and value capture alignment in business model innovation: A process view on outcome-based business models. *Journal of Product Innovation Management, 37*, 158–183. https://doi.org/10.1111/jpim.12516

Strobel, G. (2021). Information Systems in the era of the internet of things: A domain-specific modelling language. In T. Bui (Ed.), *Proceedings of the 54th Hawaii International Conference on System Sciences*. Hawaii International Conference on System Sciences.

Szopinski, D., Schoormann, T., John, T., Knackstedt, R., & Kundisch, D. (2019). Software tools for business model innovation: Current state and future challenges. *Electronic Markets, 60*, 469. https://doi.org/10.1007/s12525-018-0326-1

Terzi, S., Bouras, A., Dutta, D., Garetti, M., & Kiritsis, D. (2010). Product lifecycle management– From its history to its new role. *IJPLM, 4*, 360. https://doi.org/10.1504/IJPLM.2010.036489

Tesch, J. F., Brillinger, A.-S., & Bilgeri, D. (2017). Internet of things business model innovation and the stage-gate process: An exploratory analysis. *International Journal of Innovation Management., 21*, 1740002. https://doi.org/10.1142/S1363919617400023

Turber, S., Vom Brocke, J., Gassmann, O., & Fleisch, E. (2014). Designing business models in the era of internet of things. In D. Hutchison, T. Kanade, J. Kittler, J. M. Kleinberg, A. Kobsa, F. Mattern, J. C. Mitchell, M. Naor, O. Nierstrasz, C. Pandu Rangan, B. Steffen, D. Terzopoulos, D. Tygar, G. Weikum, M. C. Tremblay, D. VanderMeer, M. Rothenberger, A. Gupta, & V. Yoon (Eds.), *Advancing the impact of design science: Moving from theory to practice* (Vol. 8463, pp. 17–31). Springer International Publishing.

Turetken, O., Grefen, P., Gilsing, R., & Adali, O. E. (2019). Service-dominant business model Design for Digital Innovation in smart mobility. *Business and Information Systems Engineering, 61*, 9–29. https://doi.org/10.1007/s12599-018-0565-x

Vargo, S. L., & Clavier, P. (2015). Conceptual framework for a service-ecosystems approach to project management. In *2015 48th Hawaii international conference on system sciences* (pp. 1350–1359). IEEE.

Verdugo Cedeño, J. M., Papinniemi, J., Hannola, L., & Donoghue, I. (2018). Developing smart services by internet of things in manufacturing business. *dtetr*. https://doi.org/10.12783/dtetr/icpr2017/17680

Vink, J., Koskela-Huotari, K., Tronvoll, B., Edvardsson, B., & Wetter-Edman, K. (2021). Service ecosystem design: Propositions, process model, and future research agenda. *Journal of Service Research, 24*, 168–186. https://doi.org/10.1177/1094670520952537

Wieland, H., Hartmann, N. N., & Vargo, S. L. (2017). Business models as service strategy. *Journal of the Academy of Marketing Science, 14*, 3. https://doi.org/10.1007/s11747-017-0531-z

Zolnowski, A. (2015). *Analysis and design of service business models*. Dissertation, Universität Hamburg.

Zolnowski, A., Christiansen, T., & Gudat, J. (2016). Business model transformation patterns of data-driven innovations. In *Proceedings of the 24th European Conference on Information Systems*.

Zott, C., Amit, R., & Massa, L. (2011). The business model: Theoretical roots, recent development, and future research. *Journal of Management, 37*, 1019–1042. https://doi.org/10.1177/0149206311406265

Chapter 4
Research Approach

4.1 Overview

Building on the conceptual foundations presented in the previous section, a combination of research methods was applied to address the defined research objectives. As shown in Fig. 4.1, the research strategy builds on two main approaches:

- *Empirical research* on the processes of developing service systems can provide valuable insights to inform SSE (Böhmann et al., 2014). Here, it is applied to understand how SSI projects are organized and conducted in practice. Data are gathered through interviews with industry experts and analyzed using qualitative content analysis. These findings serve as a foundation for conceptualizing mechanisms such as the dynamics of actor-role assignments across different ecosystem states or iterative uncertainty reduction. Additionally, a case study helped to evaluate the suitability of LML to describe the emerging smart service system.
- *Design science research* (DSR) aims to develop novel artifacts to improve practices and performances (Hevner et al., 2004). DSR has been identified as particularly suitable for research in SSE (Böhmann et al., 2014) as it creates design knowledge and thus advances models, methods, and artifacts of SSE. DSR was applied to design a combination of methods from different disciplines that support SSI. Additional artifacts were developed for the design-integrated assessment of services and their business models. These are meta-models to capture the relevant aspects, methods for calculating assessment results, and tools as instantiations of these concepts. Tool prototypes were used to show the applicability and evaluate the utility of the developed artifacts.

The following section briefly describes how the selected research methods were applied.

© The Author(s), under exclusive license to Springer Nature Switzerland AG 2023
J. Anke, *Smart Service Innovation*, SpringerBriefs in Information Systems,
https://doi.org/10.1007/978-3-031-43770-0_4

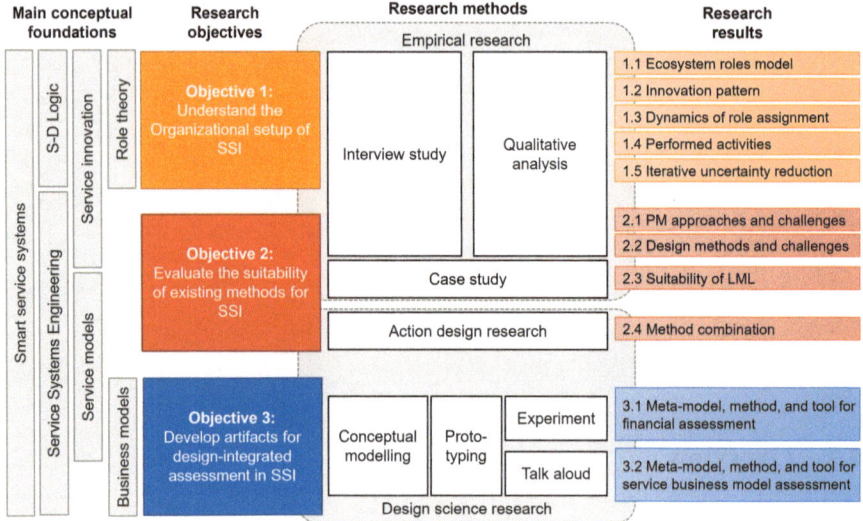

Fig. 4.1 Overview of the research approach

4.2 Interview Study

Given the need for more theoretical and empirical work on smart service innovation
(Djellal & Gallouj, 2018), an explorative approach to gathering insights on the
organizational setup of SSI appears appropriate. It was decided to use an *interview
study* with experts who participated in real-world SSI projects. Table 4.1 provides an
overview of the conducted interviews, including the experts' roles and a description
of their organization. As an indication of the company size, we provide their number
of employees in the following five categories: A: <50; B: 51–250; C: 251 to
1000; D: 1001 to 10,000; E: >10,000.

The interview study consisted of two rounds: In the first round, 14 interviews
were conducted to gather insights from specific projects, particularly on the participating actors, addressed tasks, employed means, and challenges. In the second
round, 11 additional interviews focused on the experience that experts had with
SSI in general, i.e., without restriction to a specific project. The interviews were
structured along the guidelines shown in Table 4.2 and lasted, on average, one hour.

4.3 Qualitative Data Analysis

The resulting interview recordings were transcribed and analyzed using *qualitative
content analysis*. As the first round of interviews had the character of a multi-case
study, the approach proposed by (Yin, 2018) was used for the analysis. The main
aspects of each project, along with the main sections of the interview guidelines,

Table 4.1 Overview of expert interviews

Organization description (size category)	Expert position in organization	Interview duration (2018)	Interview duration (2020)
Digital platform provider for energy management (B)	Head of product management	1:30 h	1:05
Insurance company (E)	Project manager	1:04 h	1:35 h
Utilities and public transport (C)	Project manager	1:29 h	−/−
Global IT solution provider (E)	IT architect and consultant	1:17 h	1:43 h
	Program manager	1:27 h	−/−
Digital platform provider for energy trading (C)	Project manager	1:11 h	1:41 h
IT solution provider, consulting, software development (B)	Lead architect	1:13 h	−/−
IT consulting (D)	Program manager	0:41 h	1:24 h
IT and digital business solution provider (D)	Member of the project steering board	1:06 h	−/−
Management consulting for utilities (B)	Team Lead for digitalization and IT	1:14 h	−/−
Machinery construction for the pharmaceutical industry (C)	Product manager for service/support	0:48 h	−/−
	Chief innovation architect	−/−	1:03 h
	Head of digital solutions	−/−	0:40 h
Plant construction for packing food/non-food items (B)	Head of after sales service	0:41 h	1:03 h
Internal IT providers (two different entities) of a large machinery manufacturer (D)	IT solution consultant	1:00 h	−/−
	Project manager	−/−	1:13 h
	Data scientist		
	UX designer	−/−	0:49 h
Provider of field service management software (A)	CEO	1:04 h	1:00 h

were captured in case summaries. As three researchers were involved in this analysis, their individual findings were compared and consolidated. From these consolidated case summaries, the following aspects were extracted:

- Involved actors and their contributions
- Project management approaches
- Applied means for service design, i.e., for development and documentation
- Challenges in project management and service design

Table 4.2 Abridged interview guidelines

Interview guideline in 2018	Interview guideline in 2020
1. Introduction of interviewer and expert, description of the expert's organization, expert's background, and his/her role in the organization 2. Identification of smart service innovation projects, in which the expert was involved, and selection of one project for closer analysis in the following sections of the interview 3. Project initiation, including a general description of the project and the trigger for starting the project 4. Project organization, including internal and involved external actors, the project management approach, employed methods, and specifications made 5. Project outcome, including the value proposition, operational process design, and resource configuration of the smart service system	1. Follow-up on the previous interview including a brief retrospective on the specific project from the initial interview 2. Actors and roles that can be present in smart service innovation projects 3. Multi-actor project management including methodologies, collaborative tools, and distribution/coordination of work across actors/roles 4. Methods, techniques, and practices that are commonly used in smart service innovation projects

The analysis results were then compiled into overviews and structured into a set of contributions by actors, methods, notations, and challenges. The interpretation of these findings resulted in the conceptualization of a set of ecosystem actors (1.1), innovation patterns (1.2), the explanation of changing actor-role assignments in different ecosystem states (1.3), applied means for project management (2.1), and service design (2.2) along with their associated challenges.

The sample was extended by 11 interviews from the second round. A broader approach was chosen to gain insight into the experiences that experts made regarding SSI across various projects. The analysis and interpretation of this interview data were performed according to the methodology proposed by Gioia et al. (2013) as an approach to grounded-theory-based interpretive research. This resulted in a hierarchical data structure of 54 first-order codes, 21 second-order themes, and 4 aggregate dimensions that described the activities of actors in SSI (1.4). As an overarching core category, "iterative uncertainty reduction" was determined. In the subsequent interpretation of this core category, the multi-level framework by Storbacka et al. (2016) and microfoundations as a theoretical lens were applied. From this interpretation, the theoretical model of uncertain reduction at the meso-level resulting from performed activities of individual actors at the micro-level (1.5) was developed.

4.4 Case Study

Case studies help to explore complex phenomena in a real-world context when little previous knowledge exists (Rowley, 2002; Yin, 2018). As notations for smart service systems have barely been a research topic, insights from case studies can contribute to incremental theory development. Therefore, the suitability of the Lifecycle Modeling Language was evaluated using a real-world case. The smart service system at hand was the automated replenishment of consumables for 3D printing machines, which is an integral part of pay-per-use. The system comprises various physical, digital, and organizational elements with different lifecycles. For its design and operation, multiple internal and external stakeholders are involved. The evaluation was guided by the following process:

1. Identify the main system elements and the relevance of their life cycles.
2. Derive information needs for different stakeholders that participate in the design and operation.
3. Analyze the scenario of automated replenishment of consumables for 3D printers.
4. Model the scenario using different LML diagram types.
5. Evaluate the model based on the elaborated information needs of different stakeholders.

From these results, the suitability of LML (2.3) was assessed regarding the potential benefits that smart service life cycle models can provide for different stakeholders.

4.5   Design Science Research

DSR aims to design innovative artifacts and evaluate their utility systematically. Such artifacts are intended to improve current organizational practices and can take the form of constructs (vocabulary and symbols), models (abstractions and representations), methods (algorithms and practices), and instantiations, which are implemented and prototype systems (Hevner et al., 2004; March & Smith, 1995). Different frameworks guide the design of science research activities. Two of them have been used for research in this book, namely "Action Design Research" (Sein et al., 2011) and "Design Science Research Methodology" (Peffers et al., 2007).

Action Design Research (ADR) aims to design artifacts in a real-world setting through systematic learning from the collaboration between practitioners and researchers. ADR is organized in four stages: (1) problem formulation, (2) building, intervention, and evaluation, (3) reflection and learning, and (4) formalization of learning (Sein et al., 2011). ADR was applied to investigate the potential of combining methods from different disciplines, including those that were specifically designed for smart services but not used in practice yet. Such methods can be transferred into practice by actively involving researchers in collaboration with practitioners. At the same time, the real-world project ensures the practical relevance of the resulting method combination. This designed artifact represents organizational knowledge of how digital service innovation can be supported by existing methods.

For that, a list of 30 methods from different disciplines was created, which serves as the basis for method selection in each iteration (Table 4.3). The majority came from the methods listed in DIN SPEC 33453 (2019). Others were identified in a

Table 4.3 Initial set of methods for the ADR project

Type	Methods		
General-purpose methods (GPM)	• 5 Whys • 9-P marketing mix • ABC analysis • Brainstorming • Conjoint analysis • Environment analysis	• Expert interview • How-might-we questions • Idea contest • Interview for empathy • MoSCoW prioritization	• Nightmare competitor • Shadowing • Stakeholder analysis • Stakeholder map • SWOT analysis
User-centered design (UCD)	• Customer journey • Digital mock-up • Low-resolution prototyping	• Pains & Gains • Persona • Prototyping	• User story mapping. • Value proposition canvas
Service engineering methods (SEM)	• Customer journey mapping • Job mapping	• Minimum viable service	• Service blueprinting
Digital service-specific methods (DSM)	• Information service blueprint	• Smart service canvas	

textbook on data-driven service engineering and management (Leimeister, 2020) or contributions from recent conferences on information systems.

The ADR project was conducted in a collaboration between a university and a German software company. This company aims to expand its product range with a new smart service that supports cost estimation for automotive parts. The DIN SPEC 33453 was chosen as an overall project structure, which describes an agile process with the phases of analysis, design, and implementation (2019). The project consisted of five iterations, each with a specific objective. Suitable methods were selected and applied based on the objective and the results from the previous iteration. For the design of the final artifact, the chosen methods were extracted, the output of each applied method was identified and labeled, and the methods were connected based on their input-output relation.

The *Design Science Research Methodology* (DSRM) by Peffers et al. (2007) is a widely used approach to DSR (Fig. 4.2). It was applied in the development of new artifacts for the design-integrated assessment of services. As shown, the process is iterative as findings from evaluation and communication can (and should) lead to further development of solution objectives and artifact design.

While the DSRM process makes DSR more concrete, it does not prescribe any methods that should be applied to fulfill the individual steps. An exception is the evaluation step, where several approaches have been proposed and found their way into research practice (Sonnenberg & Vom Brocke, 2012; Venable et al., 2016). Therefore, suitable methods must be defined for all other steps in the concrete design project. For an overview, the applied methods are provided in Table 4.4, which is organized according to the two research questions on the financial assessment of smart services (RQ3.1) and the assessment of service business models (RQ3.2).

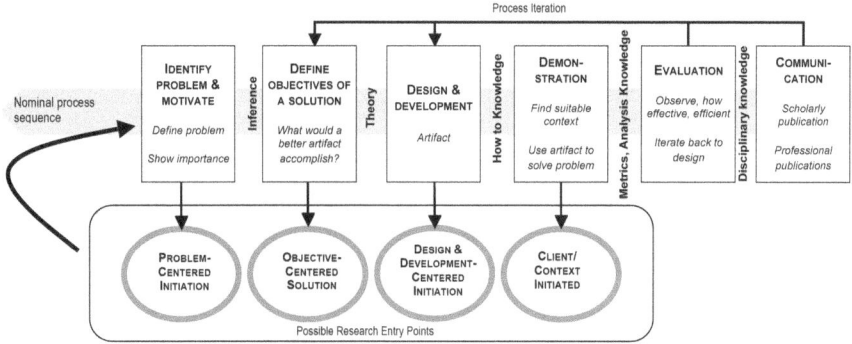

Fig. 4.2 Design science research methodology process model (Peffers et al., 2007)

Table 4.4 Methods applied in the DSRM

Phase	Smart Service Financial Assessment	Service Business Model Assessment
Identify problem and motivate	Literature review, especially on servitization and PSS engineering	Literature review, especially on data-driven business models
Define objectives of a solution	Requirement analysis based on characteristics of smart services and processes for their engineering	Requirement analysis based on business model design tools
Design and development	• *Models:* Meta-modeling based on smart service characteristics, pricing models, and financial cash flows • *Method:* Financial calculation based on techniques of capital budgeting • *Instantiation:* Development of a prototypical web application	• *Model:* Meta-modeling based on cost-benefit-analysis, effects of DDBM, and meta-model for financial assessment • *Method:* Interaction design • *Instantiation:* Development of a tool using a web-based rapid prototyping system
Demonstration	Lab experiment with 30 participants • Solved service design tasks with ideas brainstormed by participants • The experimental group used the tool • The control group used a spreadsheet	Usage of the prototype by 11 participants • Conduct nine assessment tasks • Talk aloud method during task performance • Rating through a survey after completion
Evaluation	• Apply meta-models to real-world cases • Survey of participants on tool utility	*(not conducted yet)*
Communication	One journal paper (Anke, 2019)	Two conference papers (Anke, 2020; Zolnowski et al., 2017)

The research resulted in seven linked artifacts, as shown in Fig. 4.3. The links indicate how models are used in methods and their instantiation in prototypes. Additionally, meta-models for smart services, financial cases, and business model assessment are integrated into a more comprehensive meta-model for service

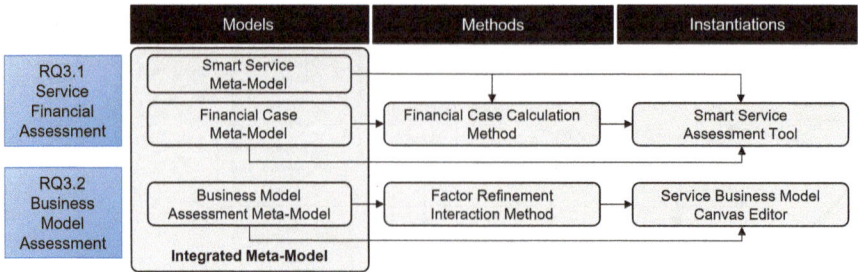

Fig. 4.3 Designed artifacts and their relationships

assessment. This integration shows the accumulation of design knowledge, which DSR research often lacks (Vom Brocke et al., 2020).

References

DIN SPEC 33453. (2019). *DIN SPEC 33453 Entwicklung digitaler Dienstleistungssysteme*. DIN.

Anke, J. (2019). Design-integrated financial assessment of smart services. *Electronic Markets, 29*, 19–35. https://doi.org/10.1007/s12525-018-0300-y

Anke, J. (2020). Enabling design-integrated assessment of service business models through factor refinement. In S. Hofmann, O. Müller, & M. Rossi (Eds.), *Designing for digital transformation. Co-creating services with citizens and industry. DESRIST 2020.: 15th* (Vol. 12388, pp. 394–406). SPRINGER NATURE.

Böhmann, T., Leimeister, J. M., & Möslein, K. (2014). Service systems engineering. *Business and Information Systems Engineering, 6*, 73–79. https://doi.org/10.1007/s12599-014-0314-8

Djellal, F., & Gallouj, F. (2018). Fifteen challenges for service innovation studies. In F. Gallouj & F. Djellal (Eds.), *A research agenda for service innovation* (pp. 1–26). Edward Elgar Publishing.

Gioia, D. A., Corley, K. G., & Hamilton, A. L. (2013). Seeking qualitative rigor in inductive research. *Organizational Research Methods, 16*, 15–31. https://doi.org/10.1177/1094428112452151

Hevner, A. R., March, S. T., Park, J., & Ram, S. (2004). Design science in information systems research. *MIS Quarterly, 28*, 75–105.

Leimeister, J. M. (2020). *Dienstleistungsengineering und -management: Data-driven Service Innovation* (2nd ed.). Lehrbuch.

March, S. T., & Smith, G. F. (1995). Design and natural science research on information technology. *Decision Support Systems, 15*, 251–266. https://doi.org/10.1016/0167-9236(94)00041-2

Peffers, K., Tuunanen, T., Rothenberger, M. A., & Chatterjee, S. (2007). A design science research methodology for information systems research. *Journal of Management Information Systems, 24*, 45–77. https://doi.org/10.2753/MIS0742-1222240302

Rowley, J. (2002). Using case studies in research. *Management Research News, 25*, 16–27. https://doi.org/10.1108/01409170210782990

Sein, M. K., Henfridsson, O., Purao, S., Rossi, M., & Lindgren, R. (2011). Action design research. *Management Information Systems: MIS Quarterly, 35*, 37–56.

Sonnenberg, C., & Vom Brocke, J. (2012). Evaluation patterns for design science research artefacts. In M. Helfert & B. Donnellan (Eds.), *Practical aspects of design science: European design science symposium, EDSS 2011, Leixlip, Ireland, revised selected papers* (Vol. 286, pp. 71–83). Springer.

Storbacka, K., Brodie, R. J., Böhmann, T., Maglio, P. P., & Nenonen, S. (2016). Actor engagement as a microfoundation for value co-creation. *Journal of Business Research, 69*, 3008–3017. https://doi.org/10.1016/j.jbusres.2016.02.034

Venable, J., Pries-Heje, J., & Baskerville, R. (2016). FEDS: A framework for evaluation in design science research. *European Journal of Information Systems, 25*, 77–89. https://doi.org/10.1057/ejis.2014.36

Vom Brocke, J., Winter, R., Hevner, A. R., & Maedche, A. (2020). Special issue editorial–accumulation and evolution of design knowledge in design science research: A journey through time and space. *JAIS, 21*, 520–544. https://doi.org/10.17705/1jais.00611

Yin, R. K. (2018). *Case study research and applications: Design and methods*. SAGE.

Zolnowski, A., Anke, J., & Gudat, J. (2017). Towards a cost-benefit-analysis of data-driven business models. In *Proceedings of the 13th International Conference on Wirtschaftsinformatik*.

Chapter 5
Summary of Findings

5.1 Overview of Research Results

SSI requires the collaboration of multiple actors that integrate their existing resources, e.g., knowledge, skills, software components, and infrastructure, to develop new resources and establish new resource integration patterns. An adapted version of the framework proposed by Grotherr et al. (2018) explains key relationships in SSI and organizes the research and its findings (Fig. 5.1). At the macro-level, smart service innovation is created by multiple actors in a service ecosystem. These actors are loosely coupled by their ability to provide relevant resources to smart services. The collaboration as service exchanges between these actors occurs within an innovation project as an institutional arrangement representing the meso-level. As different resources are needed during the project, the involvement of actors may be changed through the institutional design cycle. Project management activities are represented by the engagement design cycle that organizes the collaborative work. It includes the agreement of a project management approach and a collaborative development process. Depending on their roles and other contextual factors, actors use suitable methods and practices to perform activities toward different design objectives. These performances result in new or updated resources and patterns for their integration, which contributes to a smart service system that enables a smart service innovation with the desired value proposition.

The research and associated findings are grouped into the three aspects of organization, design, and assessment. The aspect of *organization* deals with the involvement of actors and their activities. The *design* aspect focuses on applied methods and challenges, the evaluation of LML, and the proposal of a method combination. Finally, the *assessment* aspect relates to the evaluation of smart services and their business models, which is addressed through models, methods, and tools.

© The Author(s), under exclusive license to Springer Nature Switzerland AG 2023
J. Anke, *Smart Service Innovation*, SpringerBriefs in Information Systems,
https://doi.org/10.1007/978-3-031-43770-0_5

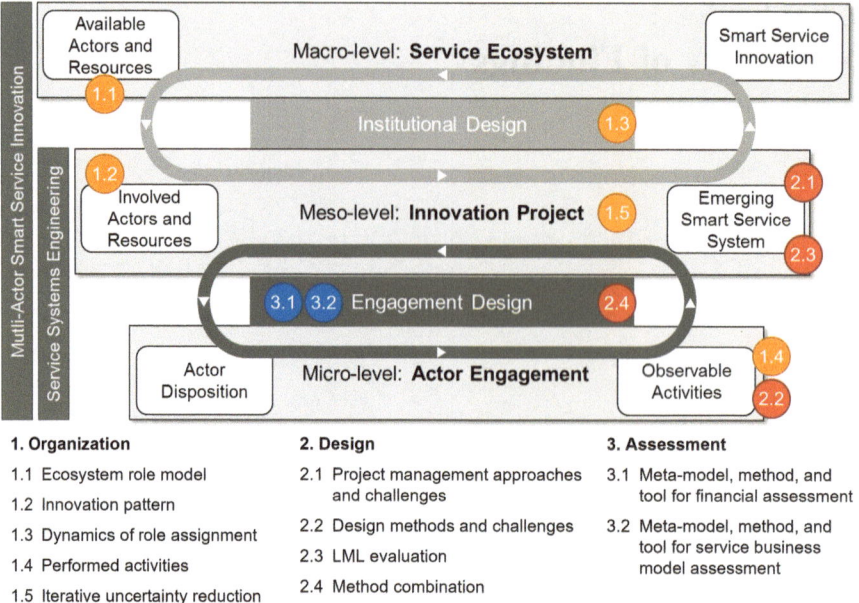

Fig. 5.1 Organizing the research and its findings in a multi-level framework

5.2 Organizational Setup of Multi-actor Smart Service Innovation

Roles of Actors in the Ecosystem

The variety of contributions from the involved actors is conceptualized in an *ecosystem role model*. It consists of 17 roles, which are clustered into Primary and Secondary Roles (Fig. 5.2). The set of roles is further systematized into different subsystems of the overall service ecosystem at different points in time. The *Engineering* subset refers to contributions needed for developing and implementing the smart service system. The *Operations* subset begins with the launch of the smart service offering into the market and refers to the actual value co-creation with the intended target group.

Primary Roles identify contributions that are required due to the characteristics of smart service systems and must be present in every project. Table 5.1 provides a description of these roles through the activities that actors with these roles perform in the service ecosystem.

Secondary Roles relate to more specialized contributions for which the demand is identified during a project. Table 5.2 shows that the respective activities range from providing knowledge on markets, customer demands, and legal advice to various technical services.

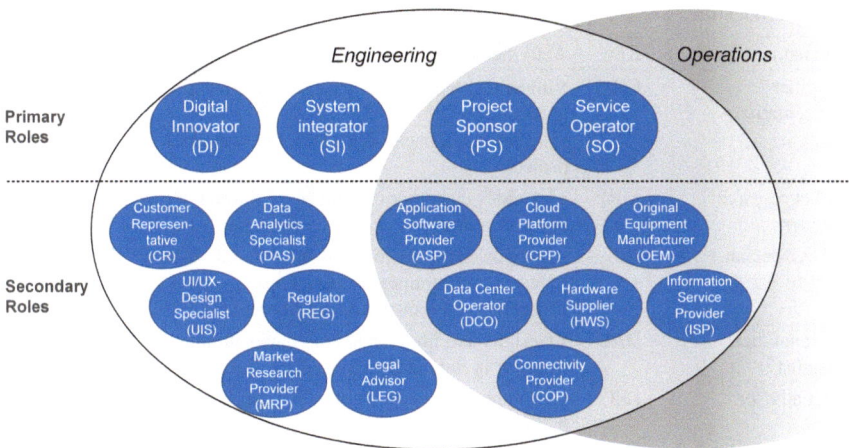

Fig. 5.2 Roles and role groups from SSI projects (modified from Anke et al., 2020b)

Table 5.1 Identified Primary Roles in SSI projects

Role name	Key	Activities in the service ecosystem
Project sponsor	PS	• Initiates, sponsors, and often manages the overall project • Operates and offers the service to the service beneficiary after completion of the SSI project
Digital innovator	DI	• Provides methodological support for the innovation process • Facilitates the creation of service ideas • Designs business model
System integrator	SI	• Develops technical concept, e.g., system architecture • Develops front-end, e.g., apps, and backend services, e.g., cloud analytics and other software components • Integrates existing systems, services, and devices
Service operator	SO	• Operates the technical part of the smart service system • Performs application management, e.g., ensures the availability and compliant operations of the system

Dynamics of Actor-Role Assignments

The need for specific competencies at different stages of innovation causes *dynamics of roles and their assignment to actors* in the service ecosystem that includes both the participation of actors and the changing roles of actors over time. The ecosystem states proposed by Edvardsson et al. (2018) are used to conceptualize this dynamic (Fig. 5.3). In the "initiating" state of the ecosystem, one actor decides to develop a new value proposition for a particular target customer group. For that, various resources, e.g., infrastructure and knowledge, are needed, as indicated by the roles highlighted as "required." By involving actors that provide the required resources, they assume their respective roles. With that, the project is enacted and transits the ecosystem to the "realizing" state.

Table 5.2 Identified Secondary Roles in SSI projects

Role name	Key	Activities in the service ecosystem
Customer representative	CR	• Informs the project as a target customer about suitable value propositions • Provides feedback during development at various stages of the project
Market research provider	MRP	• Provides customer insights, e.g., through a collection of feedback on prototypes or service concepts
UI/UX specialist	UIS	• Designs customer journey and user interactions • Designs wireframes and mockups • Supports implementation of frontends
Data analytics specialist	DAS	• Designs and implements big data solutions • Expert in data analysis, machine learning, etc.
Legal advisor	LEG	• Provides advice regarding legal aspects of services and contractual relationships between actors
Regulator	REG	• Evaluates and approves service concepts regarding their compliance with regulatory requirements
Original equipment manufacturer	OEM	• Designs and produces physical products and equipment that are part of the service system
Hardware supplier	HWS	• Supplies sensors, communication modules, and other hardware components
Connectivity provider	COP	• Provides services for connecting smart products in the field, e.g., cellular networks
Cloud platform provider	CPP	• Provides application-independent functionality in the cloud, i.e., in a platform-as-a-service model (PaaS), often with a focus on IoT
Data center operator	DCO	• Provides and operates IT infrastructure, e.g., computation, storage, and network transfer
Application software provider	ASP	• Develops and/or runs existing application software systems that must be integrated
Information service provider	ISP	• Provides information for data-driven value creation, e.g., weather forecasts, energy prices

The project acts as an institutional arrangement that facilitates service exchange between the actors. Such exchanges create new resources, e.g., software components, business models, or data analysis models. As a result of service exchanges, the new smart service system emerges. It aims to enable value co-creation in a configuration of actors whose contributions are described using roles from the operation subset. The involvement of actors with suitable resources to fulfill the designated roles enacts the smart service system and changes the ecosystem state to "outcoming." This state indicates that the service system is ready to integrate resources from the target customers and co-create the envisioned value proposition. It is important to note that the transition between states is fluent, as some actors, e.g., customers, are involved in multiple states, albeit possibly in different roles.

To illustrate the dynamics of actor-role assignments, the case of a fleet management and maintenance service is used (Anke et al., 2020b). As presented in Fig. 5.4, actor P4 planned to provide these new smart services around its commercial vans. At

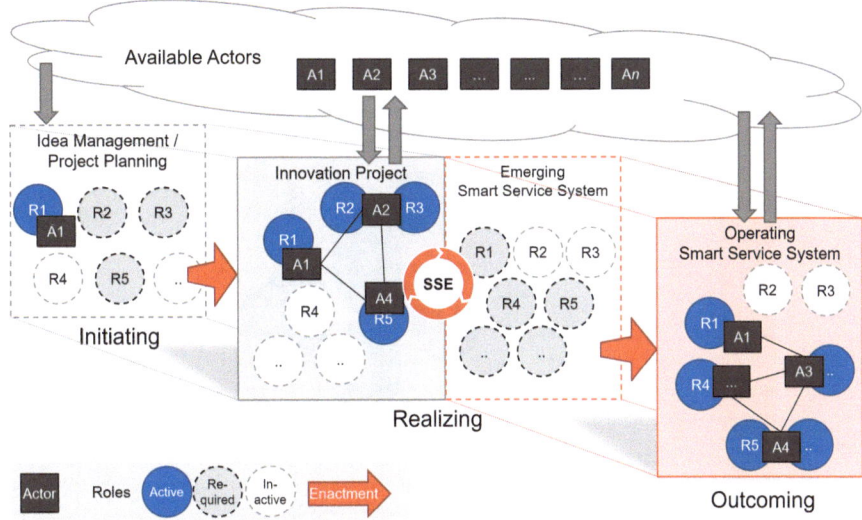

Fig. 5.3 Dynamics of actor involvement in different ecosystem states

the initiating state, P4 identified various competencies required to realize his service idea, e.g., those of a Digital Innovator, a System Integrator, and a UI/UX Design Specialist. For the transition into the realizing state, these required roles had to be filled with suitable actors. Altogether, these actors and P4 form the Engineering subsystem that collaboratively works on designing and implementing the new service idea. P4, as Project Sponsor, chose two external System Integrators (E12, E13) and hired an external design agency (E14) for the UI/UX design. An external Application Service Provider (E16) delivered the fleet management functionality. They also worked with P4 on interfaces to integrate fleet management functionality.

As actor P4 intended to use the service for its internal maintenance operations, it also assumed the role of the Customer Representative. Due to its innovation capabilities and domain expertise, actor P4 also took over the Digital Innovator role and developed the value proposition and business model. During the project, the actors determined additional competencies required for Operations, e.g., Service Operator and Data Center Operator. The launch of the service offering marks the transition to the outcoming state. For that, the required roles of Data Center Provider and Service Operator had to be filled with actors. In this case, parts of the systems were operated and managed by actor P4 itself and other components by E12. Therefore, these two actors shared the roles of Service Operator and Data Center Operator. In the outcoming state, some of the roles from the realizing state became inactive as they finished their work on the project.

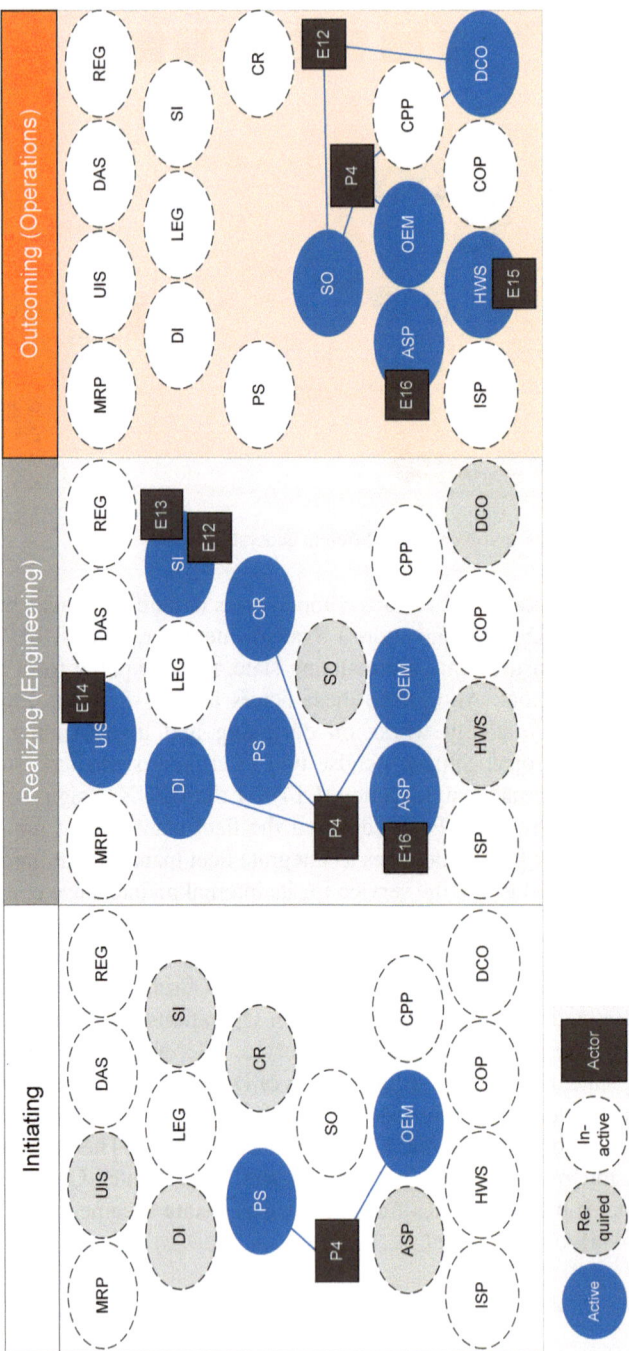

Fig. 5.4 Actor-role assignments in different states of service innovation (modified from Anke et al., 2020b)

Smart Service Innovation Patterns

The example above shows that relevant resources regarding knowledge of markets, IT, and digital innovation are distributed among the project participants. In the analysis of actor-role assignments and a reflection of the underlying dynamics during the service innovation processes, four typical constellations are identified that are called *smart service innovation patterns*. These are *Provider-driven development, Joint development, White Label Solution*, and *Forward Integration* (Table 5.3). These patterns indicate a specific strategic setup of an SSI project and the associated distribution of the business risk. Patterns also allow the analysis and design options of existing service ecosystems, e.g., regarding potential setups under given

Table 5.3   Smart service innovation patterns (based on Anke et al., 2020b)

Name	Characteristics
Provider-driven development	• Service innovation at the provider organization with the designated service provider role, possibly in collaboration with (future) customers • IT-related competencies are often not available internally • High dependency on external knowledge, especially from IT provider organizations (system integrator role), who are only responsible for the technical implementation • Provider organization needs strong innovation and project management capabilities • Entrepreneurial risk at the provider organization
Joint development	• Service innovation is driven by a provider organization together with an external actor with the system integrator role • Both actors assume the digital innovator role together • Lower requirements for innovation and project management capabilities at the provider organization due to external support • Entrepreneurial risk at the provider organization
White label solution	• An actor with strong IT capabilities (i.e., an IT provider organization) develops, builds, and runs an innovative value proposition on its own • The IT provider organization offers a white-label solution for a common problem to (multiple) provider organizations • Provider organizations assume the service provider role and market the value proposition to their customers, i.e., they offer services with minimal effort for new service development • The IT provider organization often follows a platform approach to provide customizable solutions for different provider organizations using reusable building blocks • Entrepreneurial risk shared between IT provider organization and provider organization.
Forward integration	• IT provider organization develops, runs, and offers smart service systems by itself • This actor covers most of the relevant roles through internal resources and competencies • The actor may target markets of former customers • Entrepreneurial risk is at the IT provider organization

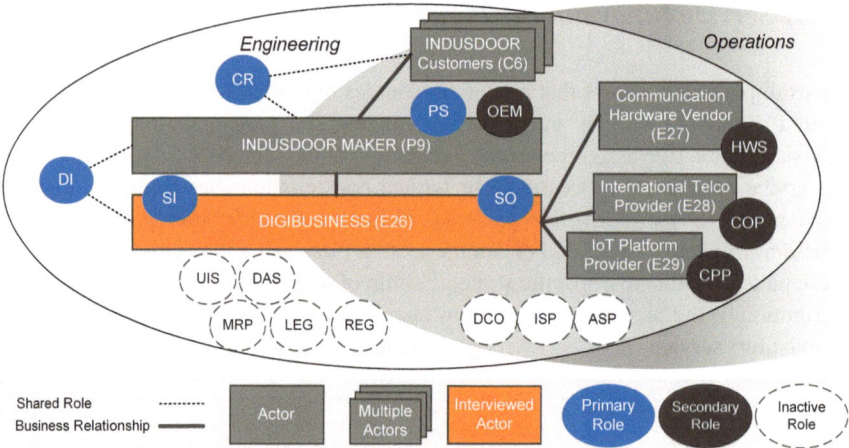

Fig. 5.5 Example of the joint development pattern (Anke et al., 2020b)

competencies per organization. They also might help to derive strategic objectives regarding the establishment of new competencies or strategic alliances with key partners.

In the example provided in Fig. 5.3, the project sponsor and future service provider develop the future services for its own products, while the technical implementation of the systems is sourced out to system integrators. Therefore, it exemplifies the "Provider Driven Development" Pattern. A different situation is shown in Fig. 5.5. Here, the digital services are developed by the project sponsor together with an external digital business consultancy. Hence, it can be classified as "Joint Development."

Iterative Uncertainty Reduction Through Collaboration

Due to the characteristics of both the type of system and the development process, actors involved in SSI are confronted with uncertainty and complexity. Uncertainty mainly relates to the multi-actor nature of SSI, where the outcome in terms of changes to the smart service system is difficult to predict. Therefore, smart service innovation uncertainty is a property of the meso-level, which refers to both the actor-to-actor network within a project and the smart service system with its changed resource integration patterns as the outcome. Actors influence future innovation activities by deciding what needs to be done in the project and who takes over responsibilities for work packages, e.g., by assigning tasks or subcontracting additional actors. Hence, the resource integration patterns of the project, understood as actor-generated institutions (Vargo & Lusch, 2016), change through the joint project work, too.

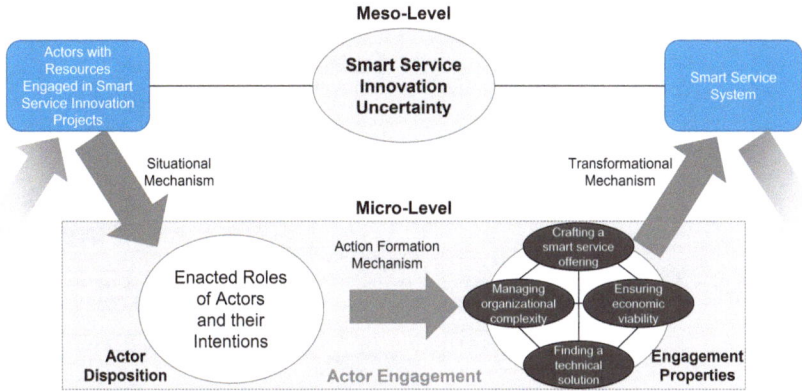

Fig. 5.6 Theoretical model of iterative uncertainty reduction in smart service innovation (Pöppelbuß et al., 2022)

The theoretical model of *iterative uncertainty reduction* (Fig. 5.6) aims to explain the behavior of actors in SSI projects to handle uncertainty (Pöppelbuß et al., 2022). Considering the current conditions of uncertainty relevant to a project, the involved actors perform activities generating a new configuration of resources which is usually supposed to reduce uncertainty. The project setup provides the conditions for actor engagement on the micro-level (situational mechanism), which influences the intentions and the roles that the actors enact during project work as actor dispositions. They are turned into action in the specific project context (action-formation mechanism). The collective action of all actors leads to the emergence of a new smart service system or changes to an existing smart service system (transformational mechanism), which can, in turn, be the outset of future innovation activities, as reflected by the fading arrows in Fig. 5.6.

The theoretical model conceptualizes the actor's activities as engagement properties. The connections between these activities emphasize that they are interdependent. For example, involving users as part of *exploring and empathizing* causes additional *multi-actor complexity* that needs to be managed. Similarly, the design of a particular *technical solution* requires specialists to be involved in the project but also influences the *economic viability* of the overall service system. Furthermore, the technical solutions are dependent on the service offering to be delivered. The interdependencies are not limited to the micro-level, but also affect the actor-to-actor network of the project on the meso-level and, hence, the smart service innovation uncertainty as a property of that level.

The main *activities that actors perform* to carry out smart service innovation together successfully are (1) *managing multi-actor complexity*, (2) *crafting a smart service offering*, (3) *developing a technical solution*, and (4) *ensuring economic viability*. These activities are conducted by different actors who assume the roles of the Project Sponsor, the Digital Innovator, and the System Integrator. Furthermore, actors with the Customer Representative role also appeared to contribute to smart service innovation, which reflects customer involvement as a key characteristic of

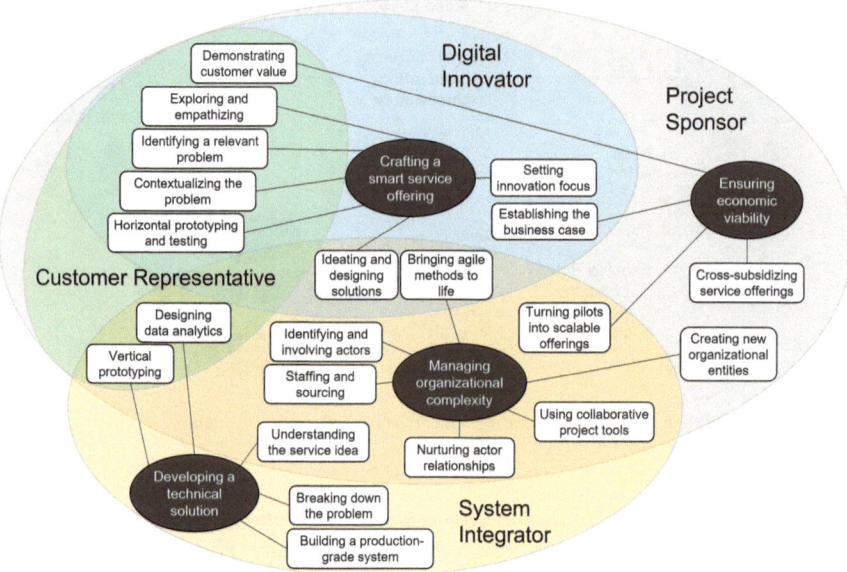

Fig. 5.7 Activities of main roles in smart service innovation (Pöppelbuß et al., 2022)

agile project management approaches. As shown in Fig. 5.7, these main activities are aggregated from various sub-activities. In line with the expected high degree of collaboration, these are performed jointly by multiple actors. For example, the sub-activity "identifying a relevant problem" is conducted by the Digital Innovator together with the Customer Representative and the Project Sponsor. Other sub-activities are done by single actors, e.g., "Creating new organizational entities" (Project Sponsor) or "Building a production-grade system" (System Integrator). In contrast, "Bringing agile methods to life" and "Ideating and designing solutions" require the collaboration of all four roles, which underlines the importance of these activities.

While the activities and sub-activities describe *what* is being done by *whom*, it does not state *how* these activities are conducted in SSI projects. This aspect is covered in the next section, which reports on the results regarding the suitability of methods for SSI and how they can be combined.

5.3 Conducting Smart Service Innovation Projects

Collaborative Development Approach

The organization of SSI projects requires agreement on how the collaborative work is to be organized and performed. For that, the organizational setup, the development

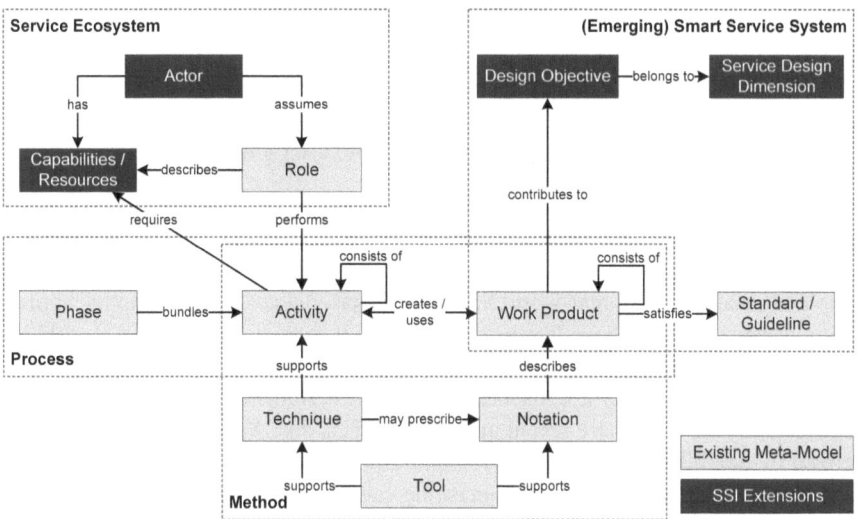

Fig. 5.8 Extended conceptual model for multi-actor service systems innovation processes

process, methods, and the (emerging) service system need to be linked. These connections are represented based on an extended version of a generic software lifecycle meta-model presented in sect. 5.3 (Fig. 5.8). In this conceptualization, the process is a sequence of activities that are bundled into phases. The performance of activities uses and/or creates new work products, which represent the current state of the service system regarding a specific design objective. Methods are linked to activities by proposing techniques for performing activities and notations for work products. Roles describe a set of resources or capabilities that are required to perform different activities (see Tables 5.1 and 5.2) in collaborative development. Activities are linked to roles, which actors assume if they possess the required resources or capabilities. The capabilities include, for example, the ability to apply specific techniques, notations, and tools to contribute to the smart service system's development systematically.

Development Processes and Project Management

As shown in sect. 5, the actors assuming key roles of Project Sponsor, Digital Innovator, Customer Representative, and System Integrator are highly interdependent. Establishing and maintaining efficient collaboration within the inno-vation process is addressed by the *"managing multi-actor complexity"* activity. It consists of various sub-activities like "identifying and involving actors," "staffing and sourcing," and "bringing agile methods to life" (Fig. 5.7). These activities are not only determining which actors participate in the project at a given point in time

Table 5.4 Employed project management methodologies

Methodology	Description	#Projects
Agile	Used an agile approach throughout the project	5
Sequential	Used a sequential approach throughout the project	4
Hybrid	The project was conducted partly agilely and partly sequentially	5

but are also setting the common ground for collaboration. Actors involved in management often have the Project Sponsor or the System Integrator roles. The empirical analysis of 14 real-world SSI projects has yielded insights into the applied methods and practices as well as the challenges in these settings (Anke et al., 2020a).

Concerning the *project management approach*, two main types were found: (1) traditional sequential approaches, e.g., the waterfall model, which focuses on predictability, and (2) more recent agile approaches, e.g., Scrum, which are characterized by flexibility and adaptability (Sommerville, 2016). If both types were used, which was observable in some projects, the category "hybrid" is assigned to them (Table 5.4). While there is almost an equal distribution of methodologies across the projects, experts who had used a sequential method often described them as unsuitable for their project in hindsight.

Additionally, experts reported on various *challenges regarding project management*, which were grouped into the categories of planning, collaboration, knowledge, and go-live (Table 5.5), along with the number of projects grouped by methodology. It illustrates the various problems that occurred in managing SSI projects. The results also indicate that most identified challenges are not explicitly associated with the employed project management approach. Instead, many challenges are related to collaboration, i.e., involving external partners appropriately, creating a shared understanding, distributing work, and receiving timely contributions. These challenges can be summarized as being related to multi-actor complexity. Furthermore, the challenges show acquiring suitable knowledge related to data-driven approaches, agile methods, software development, and modern infrastructure from external and internal sources is difficult. Notably, very few reported challenges are related to the implementation and launching ("Go-Live") of services.

Methods for the Design of Smart Service Systems

Two activities address the actual design of service systems: First, *"crafting a smart service offering"* deals with the development of a service concept that is valuable to both customer and provider. Hence, the Project Sponsor is engaged in these activities, together with the Digital Innovator, which often provides in-depth knowledge on innovation management methods. A Customer Representative must be involved in these activities if agile principles are applied. Actors of all involved roles participate in ideating and designing solutions. This collaboration highlights that the development of service concepts and their technical implementation are

Table 5.5 Challenges regarding project management (based on Anke et al., 2020a)

Category	Challenges	#Agile	#Sequential	#Hybrid
Planning	Tight deadlines; lack of time for preparation/analysis	1		
	Uncertain/inconsistent management decisions			1
Collaboration	Involvement of partners	2		
	Dependency on external actors	2	1	
	Difficulties of involving customers in an agile approach	1		
	Distribution and synchronization of work; maintaining consistency of work products	2		2
	Getting access to and aligning work with stakeholders, e.g., partners, internal units	1		1
	Achieve common understanding and a suitable level of detail			1
	Confronting functional departments with too many technical details			1
	Achieving a common understanding of concepts, e.g., industry 4.0, smart services		1	
	Work of external partners not delivered on time; threat of missing the deadline	2		
Knowledge	Need for external knowledge, e.g., software development and analytics	1	1	1
	General lack of digital transformation/innovation knowledge/skills	1	1	
	Lack of technical knowledge at the service provider			1
	Training of employees, e.g., infrastructure, data-driven approaches, sales	2	1	
	Team members or customers not familiar with an agile approach	2		
Go-live	Advancing the app from prototype status to a productive and usable one		1	
	Testing was time-consuming and required a lot of effort		1	

interdepended, i.e., service ideas are checked for technical feasibility, while technical opportunities enable new service features.

Second, *"developing a technical solution"* covers the design and implementation of the technical system that underlies the service concept. This is done by the System Integrator, a role that is often assumed by external companies. They collaborate with the Project Sponsor to understand the ongoing service concept development and work with the Customer Representative on prototypes. Finally, they are also responsible for building a technical system that is ready for productive use.

Both activities are targeted at different design objectives, i.e., the involved actors collaboratively decide on aspects of the service system. Each design objective can be related to one of the design dimensions value, process, and resource. In the interview study, a set of design objectives ("end") and the *used methods, techniques, and notations ("means")* were identified and grouped along design dimensions and design objectives (Table 5.6). The results represent the view of practitioners, which are categorized based on the aggregated responses. Not surprisingly, the responses do not always match the respective category, as terminological precision is not usually required in real-world projects. Instead, participants relied on their experience and selected means from different disciplines. By making such choices, they implicitly expressed that they consider these means suitable for the task at hand.

Working toward the design objectives mentioned above resulted in various *challenges in the design* (Table 5.7). Most of the identified challenges relate to ends with applied means. This could be due to a lack of method knowledge or poor application. In contrast, for the end "Value Capture," no means but several challenges were found. This gap is addressed by the new approach for design-integrated assessment (see sect. 5.4).

While various methods from different disciplines could be identified, there were no methods applied in real-world SSI projects specifically designed for smart services. This raises the question of how to *combine methods from different disciplines* to reuse existing methods and transfer new methods to practice (Richter & Anke, 2021). Potentially suitable methods for SSI are categorized as "digital service-specific methods" (DSM), "service engineering methods" (SEM), "user-centered design methods" (UCD), and "general-purpose methods" (GPM). Each set of methods is applicable for different purposes. Methods of the GPM category are the most general ones, e.g., from social research or marketing and management. UCD methods are often used in agile projects to ensure that users accept the resulting products. While UCD can be applied to any technical or digital product or service, SE methods are targeted at engineering services. Finally, DSM consider the specifics of digital services, such as data, devices, and analytics.

Within a real-world project based on the action design research approach (see sect. 5.4.1), a set of methods from different disciplines was chosen and combined to develop a service for "predictive costing" in the automotive industry. Figure 5.9 shows the resulting method combination. The linking of methods is organized based on the input-output-relations, i.e., a method takes the result from the preceding method as input and produces an output that fits the subsequent method. The designed method combination highlights the central role of the Smart Service Canvas (Pöppelbuß & Durst, 2019) to establish a connection between customer, value, and ecosystem perspectives for smart services. Various methods from other disciplines help to elaborate the details of these perspectives.

The method combination is by no means the only or the best possible combination. Instead, it shows that methods from different disciplines are suitable for SSI, and they can be combined beneficially. This finding underscores the reusability of existing method knowledge for SSI and the necessity to guide the selection and combination of methods for a given situation (Richter & Anke, 2021).

Table 5.6 Aggregated set of means for different design objectives in real-world SSI projects (based on Anke et al., 2020a)

	Design objective	Techniques and practices (Means for development)	Work products and notations (Means for documentation)
Value dimension	*Customer understanding*	• Feedback on current service • Customer ideas, customer as product owner • Workshops, discussions, design thinking • Internal platform (prediction market) • Expert interviews, field tests with test users	• MVP, paper-based prototypes • Epics and user stories • Customer journeys, personas • Requirement specifications
	Value proposition	• Identify/prioritize actors/customers and their jobs/problems • Understand the capabilities of existing systems as a basis for new services • Interactive discussion, workshops • Check for legal hurdles (e.g., patents, privacy, regulatory)	• Slides, whiteboards, bullet points • Textual specifications • Workshop documentation according to a structured innovation approach • Business model canvas, value proposition design, personas • Use cases
Process dimension	*User interaction/ user interfaces*	• Involvement of UX experts. • Early testing/improvement through feedback • Workshops, discussions, analysis • Definition of roles and permissions • Design guidelines	• Prototypes, wireframes, click dummies, atomic design, modular standard screens • Customer journeys, service journeys • Process models • Textual description of process steps
	Background processes	• Technical documentation • Process definitions. • Domain expertise of product owner	• Textual description • Informal modeling of process steps • Graphical models (BPMN, UML, flowcharts)
Resource dimension	*Technical concept*	• Review of existing components, compliance with existing architecture/equipment • Define new components, comply with architectural guidelines, 12-factor cloud apps • Traditional system specification, derivation of technical requirements • Iterative implementation on a test platform	• Vertical prototypes • IT architecture model, microservices • UML models • ArchiMate models • Interface definitions • User stories and epics

Table 5.7 Identified challenges in smart service innovation (based on Anke et al., 2020a)

	Design obj.	Category	Challenges
Value dimension	*Customer understanding*	*Market dynamics*	• Dependency on external developments, e.g., technological advancements
		Requirements	• Unspecific customer requests • Variety of customer requirements
	Value proposition	*Target customer* *Problem*	• Decisions on customer segment/target group • Choosing a problem, which is to be addressed
		Quality	• Deciding the level of quality of service, i.e., functionality vs. price level
		Legal	• Unclear legal conditions, e.g., on billing methods, potential patent violation, regulatory compliance, ownership of data
		Features	• Defining the feature set for the initial launch, future releases, and prioritization of necessary vs. useful features in general
	Value capture	*Revenue model*	• Distribution of financial benefits
		Pricing decisions	• Finding a good pricing model, refining the pricing model • Customers with different price expectations/perceptions
		Business model	• Difficulties in identifying suitable business models
Process dim.	*User interaction/user interfaces*	*Touchpoints*	• Unclear if additional efforts in user interface simplification will pay off • Determine the suitable number of elements should on a page, i.e., the amount of information that users can handle
	Backgroundprocesses	*Process design*	• Capabilities and degrees of freedom in existing systems had to be matched to requirements; change of either systems or requirements
Resource dimension	*Technical concept*	*System architecture*	• Number of connected products, amount of transmitted data unknown • A load-aware mechanism for data collection and transmission • Cross-system identity management. • Enabling/extending the underlying platform for new requirements. • Determining the required data and data quality.
		System integration	• Getting the system running globally, consideration of country-specifics • Integrating devices; implementing protocol adapters • Integration of existing systems; data access in heterogeneous systems

(continued)

Table 5.7 (continued)

Design obj.	Category	Challenges
		• Missing/incomplete documentation of hardware and external systems
	Technology choice	• Low maturity of the technology stack • Selection of communication technology, e.g., MQTT vs. OPC-UA • Selection of cloud/IoT-platform provider

An Integrated, Lifecycle-Oriented Model of Smart Service Systems

Smart service systems have many elements that must work together to enable the intended value proposition. Within the SSI project, development activities create and update work products that capture the design decisions made in the process. These work products represent diverse system elements that contribute to design dimensions. As shown in Table 5.6, work products are documented in different forms and notations. It illustrates the interdisciplinary character of SSI projects, where the involved actors apply methods from several disciplines.

However, this leads to two challenges: First, using multiple representations of different service system aspects results in a fragmented view of the emerging smart service system along its design dimensions. This is reflected in some collaboration challenges in Table 5.5, e.g., "maintaining consistency of work" and "achieving common understanding and suitable level of detail." Second, none of the identified notations explicitly consider the lifecycle of individual system elements. This becomes particularly relevant in later stages of the service operation, where changes in processes, updates of software components, or replacements of physical parts may impact other system elements. Making these dependencies explicit helps to manage risks by understanding the impact of changes. It is valuable for planning and conducting system modifications in a way that reduces the impact on system availability.

Experts mention using the Unified Modeling Language (UML) as a notation to describe the processes and resources of the system to be designed (see Table 5.6). However, UML does not support the modeling of lifecycles and has no built-in semantics for system elements. A recently proposed variant of the System Modeling Language (SysML) is the Lifecycle Modeling Language (LML) (LML Steering Committee 2015). It aims to support the management of complex systems throughout their lifecycle by providing a simple graphical notation and semantics to the modeling elements, e.g., asset, action, requirement, cost, and decision (LML Steering Committee 2015). LML allows the expression of both the structure and the behavior of systems through dependencies and hierarchical refinements between the elements. Therefore, systems can be viewed from multiple perspectives at different levels of granularity.

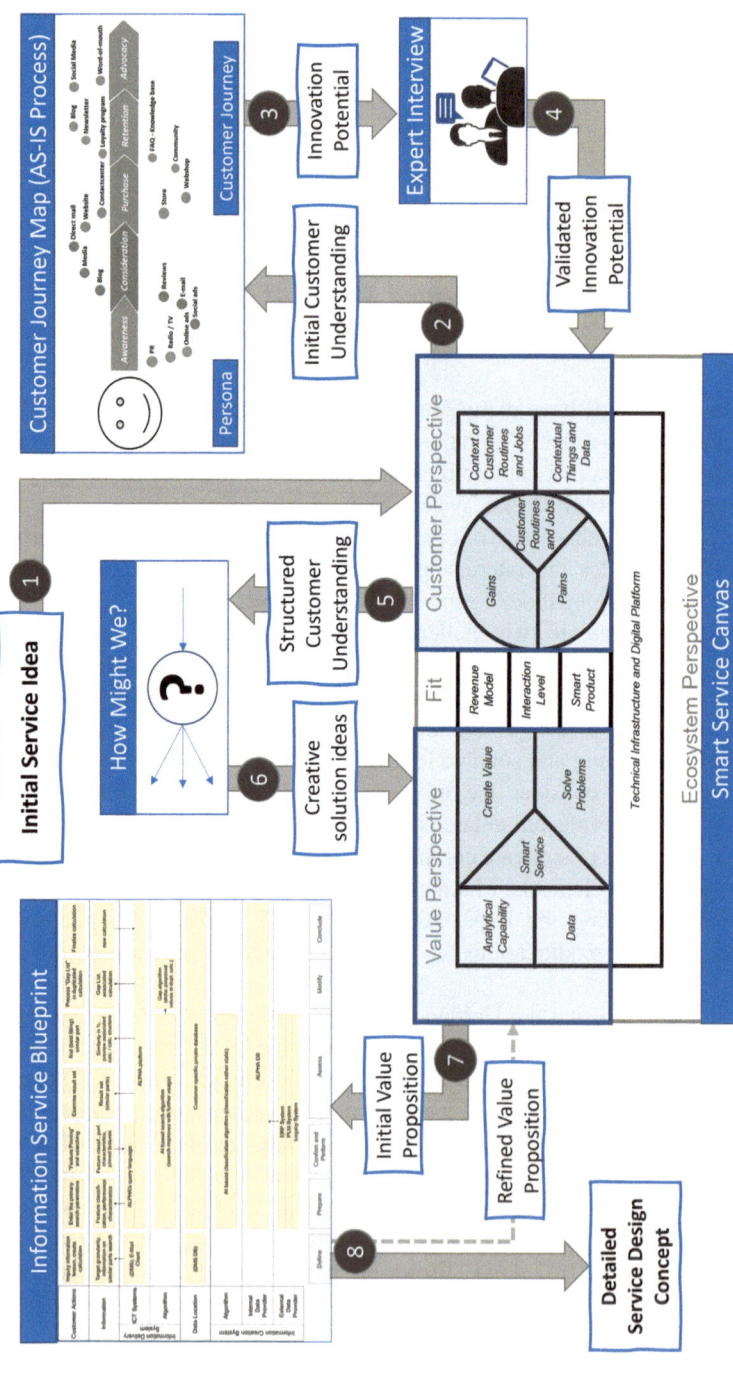

Fig. 5.9 Combination of methods for iterative service innovation (Richter & Anke, 2021)

Table 5.8 Information needs of different stakeholders by life cycle phase

Department	BOL needs	MOL needs	EOL needs
Marketing	Customer needs, prices	Customer satisfaction, customer number	Next-generation products, recycling demands
Development	System requirements, solution approaches	Identified problems and bugs	Technical migration paths to the next version
Finance	Planned revenues and development cost	Operating cost and actual revenues	Cost for warranties and recycling
Procurement	Type of items for procurement, planned lead times, potential suppliers	Quantities and times for the provision of intermediate consumption	*(no information needs identified)*
Logistics	Required stock space, lead time, package sizes, quantities	Items to be delivered quantities and dates	Removal of old equipment from customer sites and/or recycling
Customer support	Contact channels, availability, languages, response times	Current incidents/tickets	*(no information needs identified)*

The suitability of this language for modeling smart services was evaluated in a case study on the replenishment of consumables (filament) for 3D printers (Anke et al., 2018). The information demands of different stakeholders at the service provider have been identified (Table 5.8) and distinguished by the lifecycle phases beginning-of-life (BOL), middle-of-life (MOL), and end-of-life (EOL), as proposed by Kiritsis (2011).

Using a CPS perspective of this smart service system helped to assign suitable LML modeling elements, e.g., activities, inputs/outputs, assets, and conduits. A high-level model of the smart service system and its lifecycle phases with data elements and infrastructure (Fig. 5.10) was created using the Innoslate[1] tool. Activities with a "decomposed" label indicate that further refinements are available for these elements. Further refinement of elements in hierarchies led to up to five levels of abstraction in the resulting model. This facility helps capture additional details during the development of the service concept. At the same time, a good overview was still provided at higher levels of aggregation.

Overall, the evaluation of the model found that LML is a powerful approach that allows capturing of the various elements and relationships of complex smart service systems. These dependencies support risk analysis as they help to understand the effects of changes. While it allows modeling lifecycle aspects of the system, the strengths of the modeling approach lie in the collaborative design support at design time, i.e., the BOL phase. In contrast, the information needs at the MOL phase are not well addressed. This is mainly due to the lack of dynamic data that relates to individual instances of the system rather than the general system concept. Additional

---

[1] https://www.innoslate.com/systems-engineering/

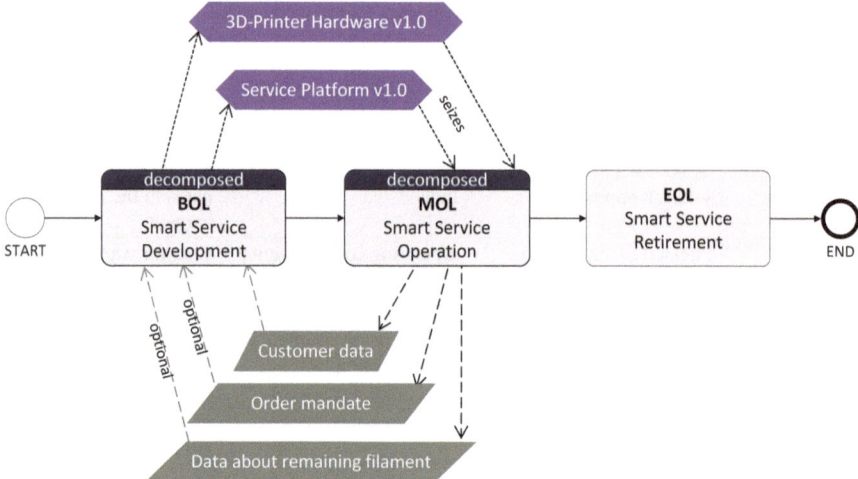

Fig. 5.10 Top-level model view of smart service for consumables replenishment (Anke et al., 2018)

tools are required to create digital twins for operational systems from LML models and update relevant attributes with real-time values.

5.4   Design-Integrated Assessment of Smart Services

Activities for Value Assessment

SSI aims to develop smart service systems that create value for the involved actors. Practitioners have reported various challenges when designing the value dimension in service systems, e.g., finding a promising target group and customer problem, distributing financial benefits, finding a pricing model, and developing suitable business models in general (Table 5.7). While customer value is often part of service design, the provider value must be separately assessed. This task is captured in the activity *"ensuring economic viability,"* which consists of the sub-activities "Demonstrating customer value," "Establishing the business case," "Turning pilots into scalable offerings," and "Cross-subsidizing service offerings." These sub-activities require understanding the financial implications that concrete service might have, e.g., in terms of expected costs, savings, and revenue. Various details like prices, usage intensity, and customer group size need to be defined to calculate these. Not all assessment-related aspects are expressible quantitatively, so strategic criteria must also be considered. However, no specific means for development and documentation were identified to support activities for designing the value capture in the interview sample (see Table 5.6). This indicates a lack of methods and tools that support the assessment of smart services and service business models.

Meta-Modeling for Smart Service Assessment

A suitable model that captures the relevant information is a prerequisite for assessing service ideas and business models. They need a common basis to support calculations and analyses on the models. This can be provided by a meta-model that acts as an abstract syntax (Zolnowski et al., 2017). Concrete models for services and their business models are instances of this meta-model. The challenge is to define meta-models in a way that balances expressiveness and simplicity. *Expressiveness* refers to the ability to capture the main elements of a service concept and its assessment-related information. *Simplicity* aims to keep the number of model elements low to make models easy to modify and comprehend. Furthermore, assessment results are sufficient to be rough estimates, as only basic aspects of the system are known in the early stages of development (Anke, 2019).

The service business model addresses the design dimension "Market" and contains the fundamental business logic of service. For the *assessment of business models*, a cost-benefit analysis was used as the underlying approach. Based on empirically identified effects of data-driven business models, a meta-model was developed to qualify each factor (which are typically represented by "post-it" notes in physical settings) on an SMBC as revenue, cost, savings, or non-financial effect (Zolnowski et al., 2017). All effects are represented by a few attributes that capture the information required for calculations.

A complementary approach to the assessment puts the service architecture in the focus of a *financial assessment of smart services*. For that, a meta-model for smart services was proposed to allow for early-stage financial assessment (Anke, 2019). The central element is the offer (the service), which multiple customer groups can consume. Functions describe the most basic features that are required to provide the service. The invocation of these functions can trigger the execution of external services or the request for data from IoT devices. Data points model the data from connected devices. Based on the amount of data needed for requests and responses, the overall data volume can be determined. As offers, functions, external services, and device data can be flexibly combined, the meta-model also fulfills the principle of recombinant service engineering (Beverungen et al., 2018). A financial case can be derived using the data provided by attributes in the model. The integrated meta-model for both aspects is shown in Fig. 5.11 as a UML class diagram.

Methods and Tool Prototypes for Design-Integrated Assessment

Based on the meta-models, two tool prototypes were developed to show the applicability of the meta-model and provide a basis for demonstration and evaluation. They allow users to create and modify models that capture the current decisions on

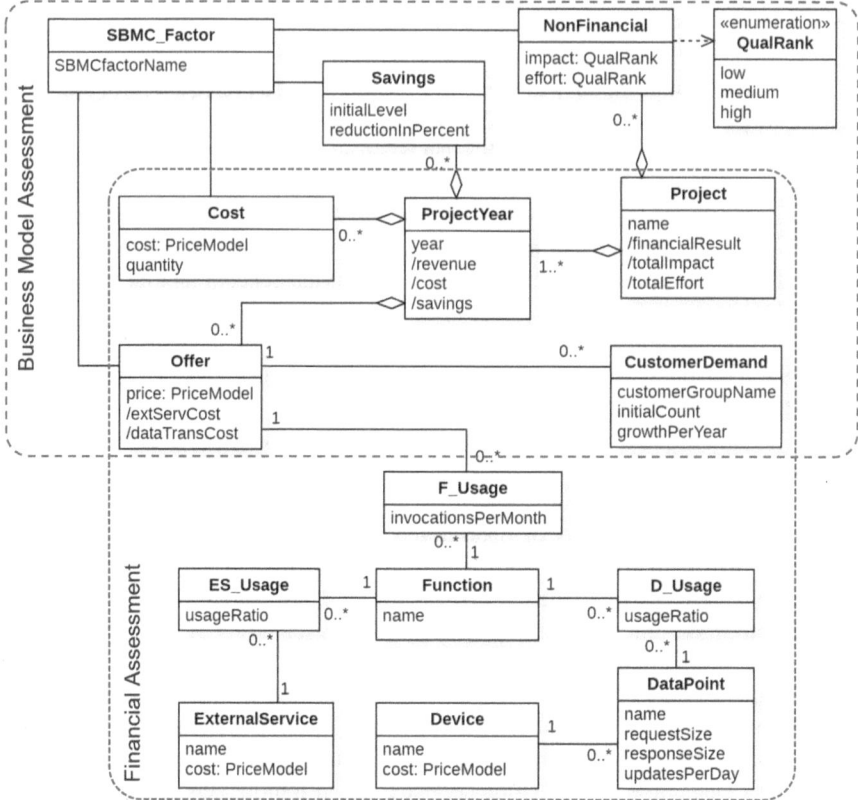

Fig. 5.11 Integrated meta-model for the assessment of smart services and their business models (extended from Zolnowski et al., 2017)

the service concept. Specifically, these tools were designed to fulfill the following requirements:

- Assessments must be possible in the early stages of the design with incomplete information.
- The addition and modification of elements, properties, relationships, quantities, prices, and costs must be possible in any order.
- The representation of models and assessment results must be comprehensible for users from different disciplines.

The *"Service Business Model Canvas Editor" prototype* supports the assessment of service business models (Anke, 2020). As business models are typically developed on a canvas-style board, the SBMC (see Fig. 3.2 in sect. 3.1) was chosen as the core metaphor for the editor. The key challenge for this task is to connect the qualitative perspective of canvas-based business models like the SBMC with quantitative assessment. Therefore, an interaction method called *factor refinement* was developed for this purpose. The user can add factors ("post-its") to the different areas of the canvas to develop the business model qualitatively. Clicking on a factor opens a dialog box where the user can categorize its impact as cost, revenue, savings, or non-financial. Depending on the choice, assessment-related information can be entered according to the attributes of the underlying meta-model (Fig. 5.12). A quick preview of the impacts of the individual factor is already given based on the provided data.

A detailed presentation of the assessment results is available in the report view, organized into financial assessment and strategic assessment (Fig. 5.13). It always contains the most up-to-date aggregation of all refinements made to the factors in the business model. The financial assessment consolidates data from factor refinements of cost, savings, and revenue types. All categories are collapsible to show or hide the individual items. The strategic assessment uses an impact-effort matrix, in which a blue circle indicates the average position of all factor refinements that have been classified as "non-financial." Users can switch back and forth between the editor view and the report view to understand better the business model they are developing for their service idea.

The *"Smart Service Assessment Tool" prototype* aims at the early-stage financial assessment of smart service ideas, which helps decide on the services to pursue further. It also relies on an editor to create and manipulate the business model and the aggregation of assessment-related information. Providing a rough financial case for a service idea can also help to justify the funding for the efforts required for the further development of the service system. The tool shows how the instantiated meta-model can describe the essential elements of a service architecture (devices, data, external services, functions, offers, and customer groups). These elements and their links are enhanced by parameters like quantitative data on prices, cost, frequencies, data volumes, and growth rates (Fig. 5.14).

The built-in *financial case calculation method* transfers the data from these model elements and creates a payment series for the desired number of planning years. Whenever the service model is changed, the financial model is automatically updated to show the impact of the changes made. For example, the tool allows defining functions that can be part of different service offers. These functions, in turn, might require data from smart products or the invocation of external services. As both data transmission and external services may incur costs, these are factored into the financial case that is calculated in the background. The detailed results can be viewed as a report showing the revenue and cost per year. The overall financial result is displayed in the editor view to provide instant feedback on changes in the service model.

Integration of Assessment Tools in the Development Process

As outlined in sect. 5.3.4, assessments should ideally be conducted as part of the development process, as assessment results may guide decisions toward better value creation. The presented tool prototypes support agile process models with short

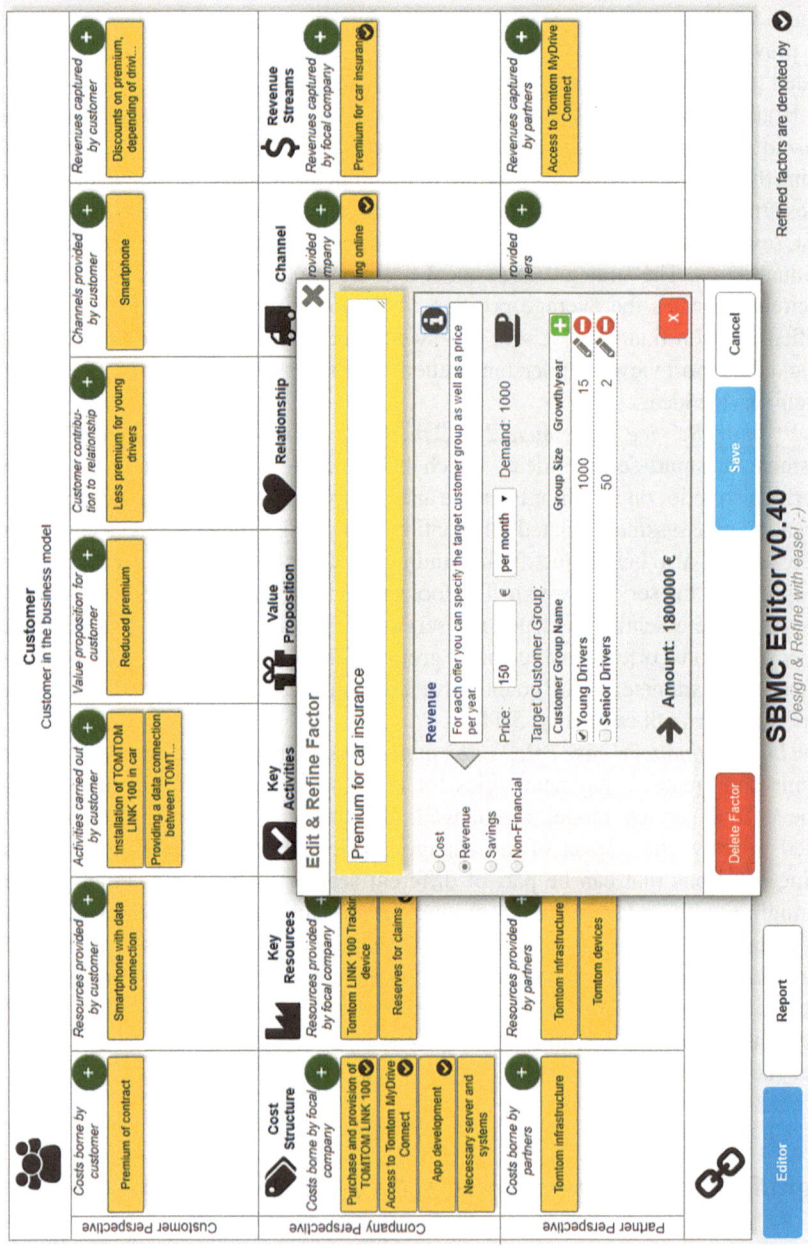

Fig. 5.12 Service Business Model Canvas editor (Anke, 2020)

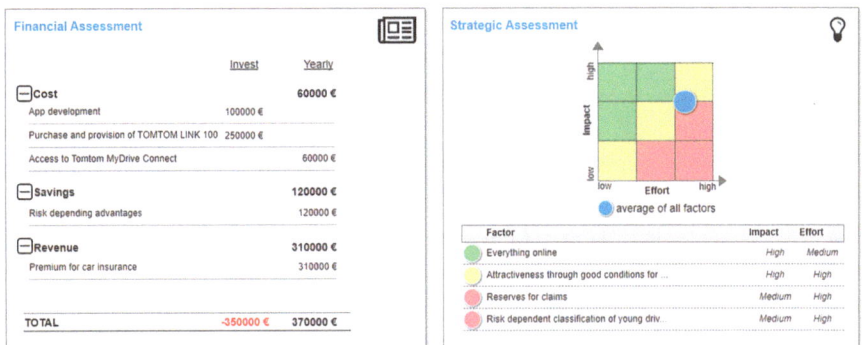

Fig. 5.13 Report view of the SBMC editor (Anke, 2020)

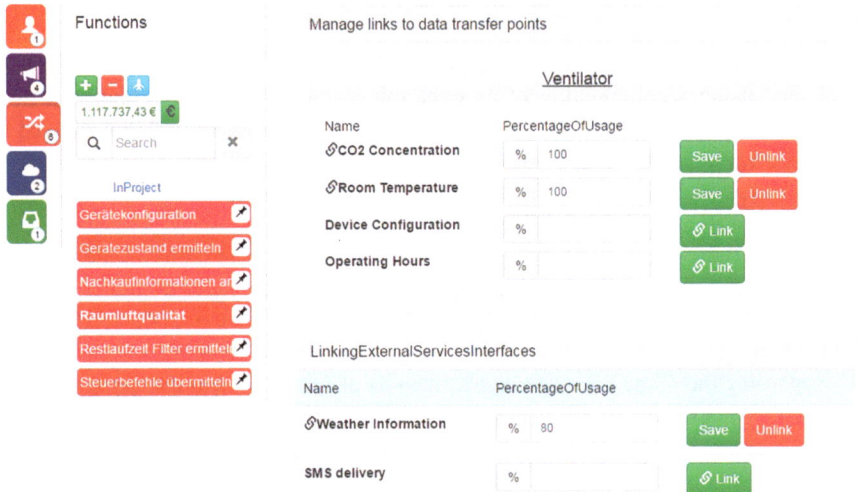

Fig. 5.14 The user interface of the Smart Service Assessment Tool (Anke, 2019)

feedback cycles by facilitating the change and adaptation of models whenever users make new design decisions. The tools are intended to be used in collaborative settings, e.g., workshops, so multiple actors to include their inputs and insights (Fig. 5.15). Tool support in these settings enables the fast and iterative modeling of service architecture and business models, including their attributes, e.g., quantities, prices, and usage behavior. Models can be iteratively modified as often as required. Each change leads to a recalculation of the assessments, which can be incorporated into the design process. At the same time, it serves as documentation of the development status over various workshop sessions, thus avoiding the loss of contributions. The iterative development is continued until the team decides to pursue or reject the service idea or business model.

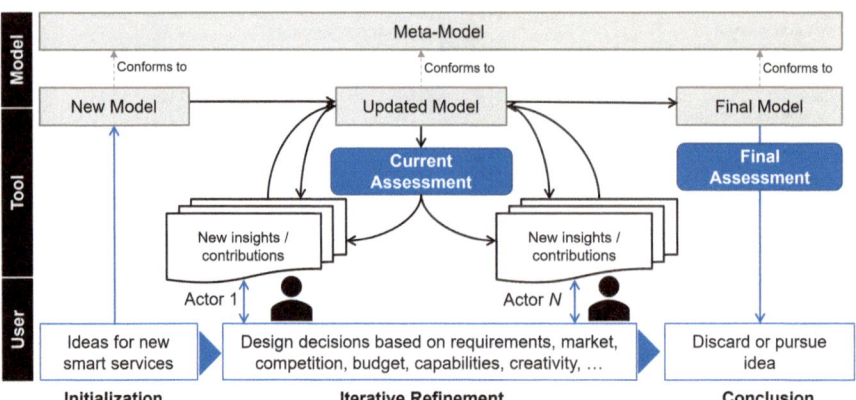

Fig. 5.15 Tool-based approach for design-integrated assessment (Anke, 2019)

The utility of these tools as an approach for design-integrated assessment was evaluated using a combination of an experiment, the talk-aloud method, and two surveys. The results for the "Service Business Model Canvas Editor" tool showed a strong indication that the tool was not only helpful, but participants also preferred it over Excel, which is typically used for such tasks. Furthermore, participants indicated almost unanimously that the assessment of business models should be tool supported. Therefore, it can be concluded that the efficacy and utility of the tool are considered positive within this sample of users. This conclusion is supported by a statement in which respondents expressed that they understood the concept of refinement.

Regarding the "Smart Service Assessment Tool," it was found that using the tool prototype is not obstructive, i.e., the tool was not hindering the design process within the experiment. Instead, participants' responses indicated that tool support is helpful, i.e., they saw a benefit of having a tool in general and perceived this tool as helpful for the task at hand. This indicates that the group of participants accepted and appreciated the general approach of the tool-based design. Structuring smart service systems based on the underlying meta-model was considered a significant benefit.

The evaluation of tools indirectly evaluated the meta-model as a central artifact. The results indicate that the refinement options are not considered too complex. However, the results also show that, at least for some participants, important input possibilities for the assessment were missing. Further research is required on whether this is due to a deficit in the model or usability deficits in the tool prototype. The presentation of reporting results is generally understood. However, the replies have considerable variance, which requires further analysis.

References

Anke, J. (2019). Design-integrated financial assessment of smart services. *Electronic Markets, 29*, 19–35. https://doi.org/10.1007/s12525-018-0300-y

Anke, J. (2020). Enabling design-integrated assessment of service business models through factor refinement. In S. Hofmann, O. Müller, & M. Rossi (Eds.), *Designing for digital transformation. Co-creating services with citizens and industry. DESRIST 2020.: 15th* (Vol. 12388, pp. 394–406). Springer Nature.

Anke, J., Wellsandt, S., & Thoben, K.-D. (2018). Modelling of a smart Service for Consumables Replenishment. *Enterprise modelling and information systems architectures (EMISAJ), 13*, 1–21. https://doi.org/10.18417/EMISA.13.17

Anke, J., Ebel, M., Pöppelbuß, J., & Alt, R. (2020a). How to tame the tiger–exploring the means, ends, and challenges in smart service system engineering. In *Twenty-Eighth European Conference on Information Systems*.

Anke, J., Pöppelbuß, J., & Alt, R. (2020b). It takes more than two to tango: Inter-organizational collaboration in smart service systems engineering. *Schmalenbach Business Review, 72*, 599–634. https://doi.org/10.1007/s41464-020-00101-2

Beverungen, D., Lüttenberg, H., & Wolf, V. (2018). Recombinant service systems engineering. *Business and Information Systems Engineering, 60*, 377–391. https://doi.org/10.1007/s12599-018-0526-4

Edvardsson, B., Tronvoll, B., & Witell, L. (2018). An ecosystem perspective on service innovation. In F. Gallouj & F. Djellal (Eds.), *A research agenda for service innovation* (pp. 85–102). Edward Elgar Publishing.

Grotherr, C., Semmann, M., & Böhmann, T. (2018). Using microfoundations of value co-creation to guide service systems design–A multilevel design framework. In *Thirty Ninth International Conference on Information Systems*.

Kiritsis, D. (2011). Closed-loop PLM for intelligent products in the era of the internet of things. *Computer-Aided Design, 43*, 479–501. https://doi.org/10.1016/j.cad.2010.03.002

Pöppelbuß, J., & Durst, C. (2019). Smart service canvas–A tool for analyzing and designing smart product-service systems. *Procedia CIRP, 83*, 324–329. https://doi.org/10.1016/j.procir.2019.04.077

Pöppelbuß, J., Ebel, M., & Anke, J. (2022). Iterative uncertainty reduction in multi-actor smart service innovation. *Electronic Markets, 32*, 599–627. https://doi.org/10.1007/s12525-021-00500-4

Richter, F., & Anke, J. (2021). Combining methods for the Design of Digital Services in practice: Experiences from a predictive costing service. In F. Ahlemann, R. Schütte, & S. Stieglitz (Eds.), *Innovation through information systems* (Vol. 46, pp. 185–202). Springer International Publishing.

Sommerville, I. (2016). *Software engineering*. Pearson.

Vargo, S. L., & Lusch, R. F. (2016). Institutions and axioms: An extension and update of service-dominant logic. *Journal of the Academy of Marketing Science, 44*, 5–23. https://doi.org/10.1007/s11747-015-0456-3

Zolnowski, A., Anke, J., & Gudat, J. (2017). Towards a cost-benefit-analysis of data-driven business models. In *Proceedings of the 13th International Conference on Wirtschaftsinformatik*.

Chapter 6
Discussion

6.1 Contributions

In this section, key findings are derived from research results and put in the context of related research. Each key finding is assigned to a research question, as indicated by its ID.

Key Finding 1.1: SSI ecosystems can be structured by a set of roles and actors that assume them by providing the resources that are defined by the respective role.

The proposed *ecosystem roles* (RQ1.1) describe typical resources that actors provide in SSI. It extends the knowledge of how technology-driven value co-creation in ecosystems is organized, as an ecosystem role expresses a set of resources that is relevant for SSI. Existing ecosystem models on this topic consider cloud computing (Floerecke et al., 2020), retail (Böttcher et al., 2021), automotive (Kaiser et al., 2021), and IoT in supply-chain management (Papert & Pflaum, 2017). As these ecosystem models overlap with SSI, future research may aim to consolidate the individual models. This consolidation will lead to a better understanding of relevant core roles for digital services across different industries, as Riasanow et al. (2020) put forward. These ecosystem models take a broader view and cover all the roles that generally exist in a specific industry or technology-centered ecosystem.

Key Finding 1.2: Innovation patterns represent typical assignments of roles to actors and can be used for the analysis and design of SSI ecosystems.

Typical constellations of roles (RQ1.2) that actors assume in the realizing state of the ecosystem have been conceptualized as four *innovation patterns*. These patterns go beyond existing research that identifies innovation patterns based on actors rather than roles (den Hertog, 2000). As patterns represent a set of roles that actors assume, they indicate the combination of provided resources. These contribute to the understanding and implications of multi-actor value constellations. For example, it enables the analysis and evaluation of the following three aspects: (1) the identification of

© The Author(s), under exclusive license to Springer Nature Switzerland AG 2023
J. Anke, *Smart Service Innovation*, SpringerBriefs in Information Systems,
https://doi.org/10.1007/978-3-031-43770-0_6

emerging business models in SSI, e.g., white-label solution provider; (2) the strategic analysis of external dependencies of organizations on external partners versus the development of internal capabilities to assume specific roles, and (3) the impact of applying these patterns for the establishment of SSI ecosystems.

Key Finding 1.3: The evolution of a service ecosystem is driven by the changing needs for resources along the innovation process, which causes actors to assume, change or leave roles.

The *dynamics of role assignments* (RQ1.3) based on ecosystem states provide a framework to align major phases of reference models with ecosystem configuration, e.g., which resources (described as roles) are required at which time and which activities are to be performed. This is in line with recent research that identifies the *distance to knowledge* as a driver for the involvement of external actors in ecosystems (Lingens et al., 2021). As the dynamics of role assignments also influence the emergence and adaption of the ecosystem structure, another perspective of roles has been established to describe the activities and influences that actors have on the adaption of the ecosystem. The actor with the strongest influence on ecosystem structure can be assigned the role of "initiator" (Ekman et al., 2016) or "orchestrator" (Lingens et al., 2021). Research also shows that ecosystems are partly emergent and partly the result of explicit design decisions (Lingens et al., 2021). Similarly, Dedehayir et al. (2018) propose a set of roles in innovation ecosystems based on the type of value contribution. The key role is the "ecosystem leader," which attracts, links, and coordinates the other actors in the ecosystem.

Key Finding 1.4: Activities performed by individual actors collectively reduce uncertainty at the project level.

The theoretical model of *iterative uncertainty reduction* (RQ1.4) identifies the main activities that actors perform in SSI projects. The model explains the interdependency between actor engagement at the micro-level and the design of the SSI project. The performed activities of actors affect not only the emerging smart service system and its properties but also the SSI project itself, e.g., by changing actors' involvement or adopting new service design methods. While the four main activities *managing organizational complexity, crafting a smart service offering, developing a technical solution,* and *ensuring economic viability* have been identified regarding their effect on uncertainty management, they are not limited to that purpose. They may serve as a foundation of a methodological framework as they also have sub-activities and relations to roles that reflect empirically grounded specifics of SSI. Developing such frameworks addresses the call for specific methods, tools (Böhmann et al., 2014), and processes (Beverungen et al., 2018) for service systems engineering.

Key Finding 2.1: Methods from other existing disciplines are generally applicable for SSI.

Conducting SSI projects requires the coordination of multiple actors. The result of their work must be integrated and contributes to the emergence of the new smart service system. To manage these collaborative efforts, various *methods from different disciplines are applied* (RQ2.1). The variety of identified methods illustrates the interdisciplinarity and complexity of SSI. However, it also shows that at least some of the existing methods are indeed suitable for such contexts, which allows reusing existing knowledge in future methodologies for SSI. This finding underlines that composing individual development methods from existing practices, as proposed by Jacobson et al. (2007), is viable.

Key Finding 2.2: Existing methods do not sufficiently address the specifics of SSI, which impedes development effectiveness.

Practitioners reported on several *challenges* (RQ2.2) in SSI projects. Most challenges are related to the complexity of multi-actor project management, the development of sustainable business models, and specific technological problems. Notably, in the investigated sample of projects, no methods were applied to support the design objective "value capture." It can be concluded that existing methods work well with aspects that are not specific to smart service systems and their innovation process. This finding provides empirical evidence for existing evaluations of methods regarding their suitability for smart services (Hagen et al., 2018; Marx et al., 2020).

Key Finding 2.3: Combining methods from existing disciplines with methods specifically designed for smart services is feasible and beneficial for SSI.

The emergence of smart service systems has led to the design of new methods and the enhancement of existing methods that consider the specifics of such systems (Marx et al., 2020). Introducing specific methods in practice is easier if new and existing *methods can be combined* (RQ2.3) in a suitable way. A working combination of methods was determined, which uses the Smart Service Canvas (Pöppelbuß & Durst, 2019) as the central element. This combination of methods builds on the ideas put forward in Situational Method Engineering (Henderson-Sellers & Ralyté, 2010) and the empirical findings on hybrid methods that combine agile and traditional practices (Kuhrmann et al., 2021).

Key Finding 2.4: LML is well suited to express the specifics of smart service systems, particularly in cases where complex smart products are designed as part of SSI.

The application of methods from different disciplines creates a variety of work results. The *evaluation of LML* (RQ2.4) indicates that it is suitable to capture the specifics of smart service systems in an integrated model, which can serve the information needs of most stakeholders along the lifecycle. This finding is supported by other research that applies LML to designing and managing PSS and IoT-based smart services (Hefnawy et al., 2016). LML is useful when new smart products are designed together with their services. However, it might be too complex if existing smart products take primarily the role of a data source. Finding suitable notations for smart service system models is an ongoing effort. For example, a domain-specific modeling language proposed by Huber et al. (2019) captures the specifics of smart service systems even better but does not explicitly support lifecycles.

Key Finding 3.1: The designed meta-model is suitable to link service architectures and business models with assessment-related information.

Activities to ensure economic viability are highly relevant to SSI. To reduce uncertainty and drive the development of service concepts, they should be assessed regularly. As the result of RQ2.2 shows, there is a lack of methods to guide such activities in practice. The results of this research extend the set of methods for SSI through an approach for design-integrated assessment of smart services (RQ3.1) and service business models (RQ3.2). The main artifact is a meta-model that captures the specifics of smart service architectures, business models, and assessment-related information. As these meta-models explicate a generalized structure of smart service systems, they can facilitate discussions on their nature and may be used as abstract syntax for domain-specific languages (Huber et al., 2019; Lüttenberg, 2020).

Key Finding 3.2: Tools for the assessment of smart services and their business models enable design-integrated assessment with incomplete information.

Prototypical *tool implementations* allow the instantiation and manipulation of models for concrete cases. As these model instances comply with the underlying meta-model, financial and strategic assessments can be continuously updated on every model change. This instant feedback is provided to the users, which may use the tools in collaborative settings, such as workshops. Implementing these tools required the development of two additional artifacts: (1) a *calculation method*, which derives financial results (RQ3.1) from the current model instance, and (2) the *factor refinement interaction method*, which enables supplementing qualitative business model items with qualitative details for assessment (RQ3.2). The evaluation of these tools demonstrated their benefit. They address the identified gap in providing assessment-related information in the design process (Turetken et al., 2019). They can improve the assessment functionality of BMDT software, which is still under-developed (Szopinski et al., 2019).

6.2 Limitations

The presented research results are subject to limitations, most of which are inherent to the qualitative research approach and the exploratory nature of this study.

- *Generalizability:* As it is challenging to access experts with real-world experience in SSI, the interviewees for the study were recruited from personal networks. While the number of experts was relatively high and covered a broad range of cases, these can neither be considered comprehensive nor representative of SSI in general. Furthermore, there was mostly only one interviewee per case or organization, which does not allow for an in-depth analysis of complex ecosystems. As the topic is broad and emerging, it is not easy to detect limits of applicability, e.g., regarding types of systems, levels of human integration, and industry specifics.

For example, a different set of cases will likely lead to a modification to the set of roles and activities.

- *Data Interpretation:* Conceptualizing and theorizing from qualitative data requires the interpretation of data by researchers, which is inherently subjective. While this was mitigated through the involvement of multiple researchers in the analysis and interpretation of data, researchers with other backgrounds may have come to different interpretations.
- *Artifact evaluation:* A large share of test persons who evaluated proposed artifacts for design-integrated assessment were students. While they do represent potential users, professionals with more experience might have given different responses. Additionally, the tool implementations were only prototypes and thus not optimized for usability. An optimized experience might have helped some of the users complete their tasks.
- *Non-normativity:* The influence of specific innovation patterns, management approaches, or employed methods on the overall project success has not been investigated. Most SSI projects in the sample were in the late stages of development or the early stages of market tests. This implies that the presented results should not be conceived as normative in the sense of common, good, or best practices.

Overall, the results are explorative and provide initial but rich empirical insights into real-world SSI projects. Future research may use larger sample sizes, quantitative approaches, and/or a more specific selection of smart services cases based on taxonomies (Brogt & Strobel, 2020) to yield more robust results. Investigating further examples of smart service innovation processes and going beyond the realizing state of such processes might lead to identifying additional roles. In particular, the outcoming state of service innovation was not in scope. Analyzing cases in the operational state will likely establish insights into the success of the respective SSI projects, including the suitability of chosen methods and practices.

6.3   Managerial Implications

Practitioners should understand that SSI projects are not mere hardware and software implementation projects but inter-organizational, collaborative, and human-centered endeavors. They must be managed accordingly, and the method and tools used in projects should promote a corresponding mindset and build suitable capabilities. The presented results are, therefore, relevant regarding (1) innovation management, (2) agile methods for service innovation, and (3) economically viable service offerings.

First, the presented roles and activities describe how actors engage in SSI and thus provide a basic idea about the necessary resources, skills, and processes for the *management of smart service innovation*. These findings guide the setup and conduct of such initiatives and highlight potential dependencies on other actors.

As SSI takes place in multi-actor settings, it is critical to identify and maintain relationships with relevant partners that complement the resources of one's organization. From a strategic perspective, the different actors must decide which resources to build up internally and which are to be sourced externally. The identified assignments of roles to activities and innovation patterns can help to analyze ecosystems and may guide sourcing decisions.

Second, the conceptualized mechanism of iterative uncertainty reduction emphasizes the importance of an iterative process for SSI. While uncertainty is an inherent part of any innovation, the awareness of the various sources of uncertainty and possible approaches to handling them may improve the innovation process (Jalonen, 2012). The experts consistently recommend the use of *agile methodologies* to reduce uncertainty gradually. They also expect that following agile methodologies increases the likelihood that new smart service offerings are designed in a way that they meet actual customer demands. However, such methodologies might be unfamiliar to traditional product-centric businesses, and employees must be trained accordingly. The presented design dimensions and objectives can serve as a preliminary checklist for the areas needing to be addressed in SSI projects. The identified means suggest potential methods that can be employed in the development process to guide the performance of activities. Practitioners should use these lists as inspiration to broaden their repertoire of methods and tools and serve as a multiplicator of suitable methods and tools through their collaborative project work. The identified challenges illustrate what can go wrong in SSI projects, providing hints for preventive action, e.g., dealing with legal issues.

Third, it cannot be overstated that smart service offerings need to solve a relevant customer problem, which is also *economically viable* for the service provider. Practice-oriented literature on business model innovation describes a continuous testing and experimentation process that distinguishes between desirability, feasibility, and viability in scaling business ideas (Bland et al., 2019; Osterwalder et al., 2020). As progress is made, the focus shifts toward assessing and ensuring viability. Hence, balancing customer needs, technical feasibility, and provider value is crucial when crafting a service offering. That is, looking at *crafting a smart service offering* in isolation only addresses the issue of "desirability." This needs to be combined with assessing feasibility to avoid putting much effort into service ideas that cannot be realized. In contrast, if services are built from a technical perspective (*developing a technical solution*) without involving the customer, the Project Sponsor risks creating a service offering that fails to address customer needs. Finally, *ensuring economic viability* is needed to ensure that costs for building and operating the smart service systems are exceeded by benefits at the provider, which can take the form of revenue, savings, or strategic benefit (Zolnowski et al., 2017). The proposed approaches for design-integrated assessment can provide practical support for considering these aspects, especially when integrated into BMDT software.

6.4   Directions for Future Research

Research on SSI is hampered by multiple theoretical and conceptual weaknesses that future research should address. These consist of (1) conceptual and terminological inconsistencies in smart service systems and their characteristics, (2) a lack of systematics in the methods for SSI and their combination, i.e., an SSI methodology, and (3) a theoretical grounding that explains the embedding of methods and processes of SSE into the organizational arrangement multi-actor SSI. In this section, these are elaborated in more detail, which includes research directions that result from the findings of this study.

Consolidate the Conceptual Foundations of Smart Service Systems

What are smart service systems, after all? While advances in different scientific communities can explain the variety of partly overlapping conceptions of the term, the often-overlooked inconsistencies limit the effective transfer of knowledge between different disciplines.

The conceptualization of the term "service system" itself has changed over time. A recent literature review by Brozović and Tregua (2022) has traced the conceptual evolution of service (eco)systems: Initially, service systems were considered in *service management* with customers, employees, resources, and technology as constituents and service quality as target outcomes. Later, the focus shifted to service systems as *value constellations* of people, processes, technologies, and knowledge that interacted to create value. In the third phase of the evolution, the *service ecosystem* notion was adopted to highlight the resource integration between actors constrained and facilitated by institutions and institutional arrangements (Brozović & Tregua, 2022). It can be seen that the second interpretation originates in service science and is used in current definitions of smart service systems, e.g., by Beverungen et al. (2019). The third interpretation is rooted in S-D logic and provides a more generic perspective of value creation in dynamic multi-actor environments (Vargo & Lusch, 2016).

Various streams of research have adopted the term service system and extended it to highlight the special type of digitally enabled services that are based on smart products, e.g., (smart) service systems, (smart) PSS, and CPS (Martin et al., 2020). The diversity of terms and meanings may lead to conceptual mismatch as the underlying definitions are not always clearly stated. Sometimes they are even used interchangeably, mainly when researchers contribute to neighboring disciplines without being aware of ostensibly subtle differences. Although each term highlights different aspects, they all share a common conceptual core that is yet to be made explicit in literature (Martin et al., 2020).

Achieving a consolidated conceptual understanding does not imply that all smart service systems should be considered the same. Instead, their characteristics should be further investigated and systematized. The current understanding of smart service systems appears appropriate for networked value co-creation. It focuses little on the engineering of the smart product, which is mainly considered a data source, customer touchpoint, or "boundary object" (Beverungen et al., 2019). Examples include carsharing, smart home solutions, and diabetes prevention. The common characteristic is utilizing (rather than engineering) existing, standardized hardware components and products, focusing on customer experience, scalable business models, and business-to-consumer (B2C) relations. In industrial domains with complex technical equipment and machinery, CPS and PSS are more often applied as a conceptual foundation. This is emphasized by transforming product-centric business models to service-centric business models through "digital servitization" (Gebauer et al., 2021). The engineering and manufacturing of the smart product is often an integral part of the core business in these cases. Therefore, product engineering aspects, lifecycle considerations, and even formal certifications are highly relevant in the innovation process. Examples include pay-per-use for air compressors, predictive maintenance for elevators, and fleet management for trucks.

To capture the variety of (smart) service systems, they should be classified based on their characteristics, e.g., through taxonomies (Azkan et al., 2020a; Brogt & Strobel, 2020) or archetypes (Rapaccini & Adrodegari, 2022). The classification of service systems is also helpful in identifying "situational factors" (Clarke & O'Connor, 2012) that guide the selection of methods based on the characteristics of the envisioned system. Understanding and structuring the varieties of smart service systems is the basis for designing suitable development methods that are "smart-enabled" (Pirola et al., 2020). The following research objectives can address these issues:

- Determine the common constituents of currently overlapping but distinct concepts, e.g., of (smart) service systems, service ecosystems, CPS, and (smart) PSS.
- Systematize the different variants of smart service systems, e.g., using taxonomies to provide a common language and reference framework for situational factors in SSI.

Develop a Methodology for Smart Service Innovation

As the presented results show, a large set of processes, methods, practices, and notations are used or suitable for the systematic development of smart service systems and related systems. Still, there is no common methodology for smart service innovation unifying existing approaches.

SSI combines digital service engineering from a marketing perspective with technical system engineering to create the underlying smart service system that enables the desired value proposition (Pakkala & Spohrer, 2019). To guide this

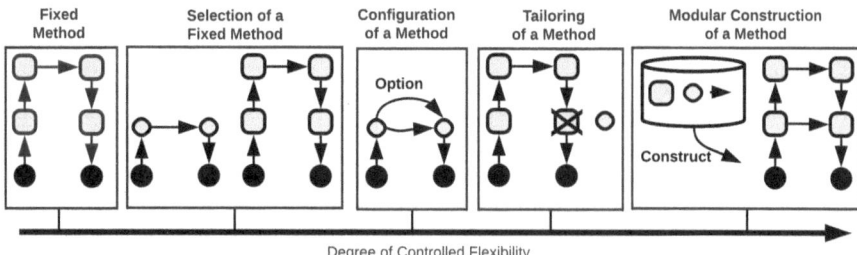

Fig. 6.1 Degree of controlled flexibility in methods (based on Gottschalk et al., 2023)

development, practitioners use many methods from different disciplines. This variety results from the different design objectives in smart service systems but also due to the variety of competence levels and professional backgrounds of the involved actors. As developing smart service systems is a relatively novel task for most practitioners, it is unsurprising that they try to capitalize on the methods they already know. While specific methods and practices are suitable for SSI, barely any identified means were designed explicitly for SSI, which confirms the findings by Wolf et al. (2020). On the other hand, Academia provides various engineering methods for software, services, PSS, and CPS, which are partly updated for smart service systems (Hagen et al., 2018; Marx et al., 2020).

The design of development processes is a field of tension between flexibility and control (Harmsen et al., 1994). *Flexibility* describes the degree of freedom in a method that allows for adaptation to specific situations during the application of the method. *Control* refers to the level of guidance in the application of the method. These lead to a spectrum of controlled flexibility, as depicted in Fig. 6.1.

Against this background, the following insights should guide the development of an SSI methodology:

1. There is a variety of smart service systems whose characteristics determine the suitability of individual development methods in a project context.
2. The different design objectives in smart services systems require an interdisciplinary approach to the development and integration of methods from these disciplines.
3. The work toward different design objectives is performed by multiple actors that need to collaborate and effectively develop the new service system.

Based on these characteristics, SSI requires a high degree of flexibility, which two basic approaches could provide for methodologies: (1) reference processes and (2) loosely coupled practices.

Reference processes are a source of information that can serve as a starting point for concrete processes. They cover many potential uses in the target domain and aim for completeness. This is achieved by a well-defined structure of work products, modeling techniques, and activities related to work products as inputs and outputs, roles, and other items. To be adaptable to concrete situations, they need to offer configuration options.

Besides the DIN SPEC 33453, which has been presented earlier, another reference process model for smart services has been proposed by Frank et al. (2020). It covers the main processes of planning, developing, performing, and billing. Each process is further detailed into sub-processes, process steps, and sub-process steps. Each of the 126 sub-steps is further described through inputs, outputs, suitable methods, and responsibilities. Depending on the level of adaptability, reference processes take the "method with options" or "tailoring a method" degree of controlled flexibility. Thus, reference process models are suitable for projects with strict compliance requirements (e.g., medical systems, safety-critical applications) and/or mechatronics systems, where it is difficult to rapidly modify physical components, e.g., industrial PSS (Müller, 2013). The benefit of reference processes is the complete coverage of the problem and the excellent guidance of users. Drawbacks include the high complexity and effort to implement them in an organization, as all participants must learn them.

The approach of *loosely coupled practices* complies with agile principles, which recommend that project teams adapt their way of working whenever they consider this necessary. It represents the "modular construction of a method" degree of flexibility. This approach requires mechanisms for the description and combination of practices. For example, SME allows reusing existing practices (or "method fragments") from different disciplines that are collected in a method base. Concrete methods are then constructed by selecting and combining these practices (Jacobson et al., 2007). A large-scale survey of software engineering in practice shows that organizations use customized methods that combine traditional and agile practices, which result in so-called "hybrid methods" (Tell et al., 2019).

In the area of smart services, Giray and Tekinerdogan (2018) build an SME-driven approach for constructing a method based on the ISO/IEC 24744 standard as a meta-model for method fragments. They show how the constructed method changes depending on the defined situation factors, e.g., team size, experience, the existence of backend services, and IoT devices. Similarly, Gottschalk et al. (2023) propose an approach for constructing a business model development method based on SME, which contains methods building blocks for the discovery, development, and validation of business models. Creating an inventory of suitable method fragments or practices can be achieved by collecting them in real-world projects, as proposed by Holler et al. (2018) for the development of digitized products, or by breaking up existing integrated methods and reference models to separate the included practices, as proposed by Jacobson et al. (2017) for IoT-based solutions.

While various suitable methods and practices exist, there is a lack of guidance for their selection and combination for SSI, i.e., an SSI methodology. Ideally, this should link the activities to be conducted for a certain design objective with suitable methods and the roles of actors responsible for their performance. To achieve that, three main research objectives should be addressed in the future:

- Identify the main design objectives of smart service systems, e.g., business model, service architecture, data analysis procedures, and customer interfaces.

- Determine a set of suitable methods and practices to guide the development activities that address these design objectives.
- Develop mechanisms that allow the selection and combination of suitable methods and practices for a specific situation.

The collaborative development of complex systems requires a consistent understanding of the current system concept, which suitable models facilitate. Some existing methods and practices include notations, e.g., service blueprint or business model canvas. While they individually contribute to the respective design objective, they lead to a fragmented model of the overall service system concept. Additionally, the relevance of managing the lifecycles of individual components in smart service systems is often overlooked, especially in the IS field. Recent contributions from industrial engineering on lifecycle management for PSS could add this critical perspective (Wellsandt et al., 2018). Modeling of lifecycles needs to be extended also to support dynamic data from individual smart product instances that cater to the needs of stakeholders for the management of the smart service system, i.e., the MOL and EOL lifecycle phases.

Future notations and modeling languages are needed to serve the demands of diverse stakeholders along the lifecycle of such systems by providing different views on an integrated model. Additionally, they should be lightweight and open to rapid changes initially but sufficiently precise for machine interpretation, e.g., in automated assessments. The following research objectives address these issues:

- Develop a concept to integrate the different views on the emerging service system concept.
- Evaluate mechanisms that enable the consideration of lifecycles, including dynamic data.
- Extend modeling languages to serve as a basis for design-integrated assessment.
- Develop prescriptive knowledge that links situational factors to the applicability of specific methods and practices.

Establish a Theory of Smart Service Innovation Grounded in S-D Logic

One of the challenges in the investigation of SSI is the lack of a conceptual link that embeds SSE into an organizational context in which multiple actors collaboratively apply SSE methods and processes. This research indicates that S-D logic is a suitable lens to explain both the mechanisms of value co-creation in smart service systems and the collaborative process that leads to its emergence (Ehrenthal et al., 2021). The missing link could be SDL-grounded conceptualization of SSI projects as institutional arrangements, in which actors provide resources to collaboratively design smart services using suitable methods and practices provided by SSE. For that, the constituents of SSI and their relationships need to be expressed in S-D logic

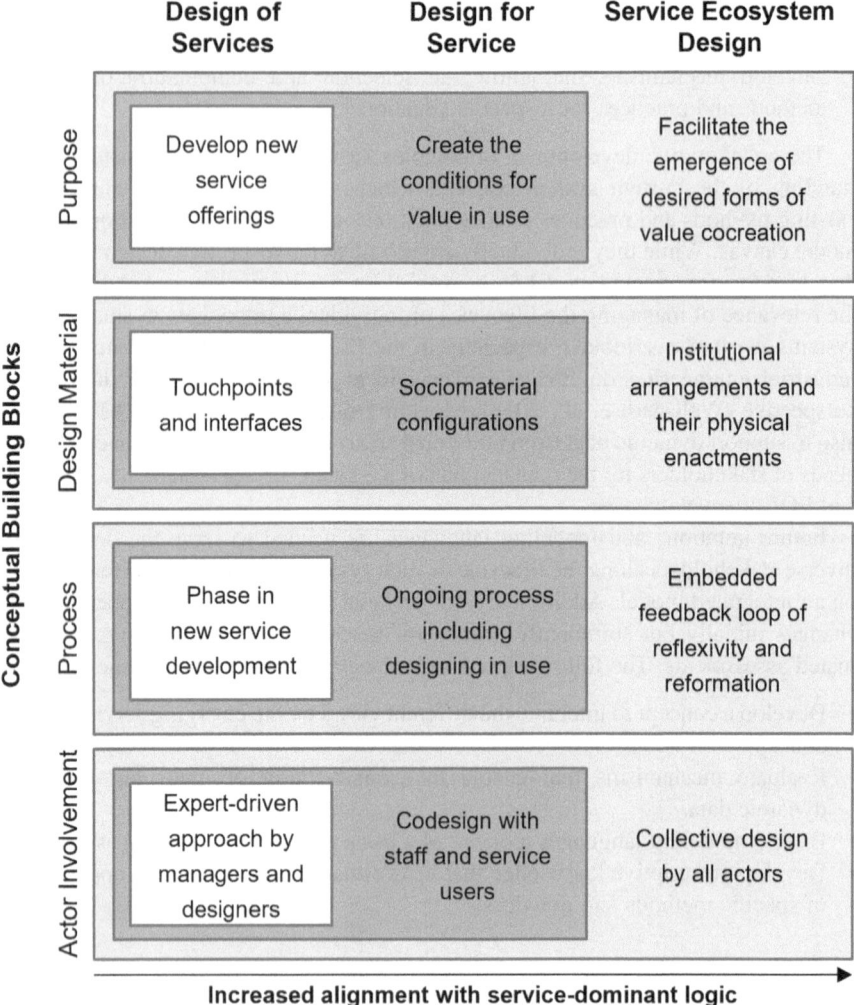

Fig. 6.2 Conceptualizations of service design (Vink et al., 2021)

constructs (Ehrenthal et al., 2021), thus allowing for embedding conceptual and empirical inquiries more holistically into this framework (Brust et al., 2017).

Various SSI-related concepts have been devised recently based on S-D logic, e.g., service-dominant architecture (Weiß et al., 2018), data ecosystems (Azkan et al., 2020b), service-oriented business models (Pfeiffer et al., 2017), and open innovation (Windasari & Lin, 2021). Additionally, service design as an SSI-related discipline has been extended toward service ecosystem design, which aligns better with SDL (Vink et al., 2021). These extensions are described by the conceptual building blocks of actor involvement, processes, design material, and purpose (Fig. 6.2). The proposed levels of alignment with SDL relate to the evolution phases of the term "service system" (see sect. 6.4.1).

In this research, S-D logic has been used as a lens to study the phenomena related to SSI. It was shown that SSI projects are higher-order service systems consisting of individual actors representing the service systems themselves. Projects can be understood as institutional arrangements, as they facilitate and constrain service exchange among the participating actors. The applied SSE methods and processes can be viewed from two perspectives. First, they are part of institutional arrangements by establishing concrete rules for distributing work and integrating work results. Second, they represent operant resources of actors as the mastery of methods requires skills and knowledge that actors contribute to the SSI project by assuming roles that represent a set of typical resources required for SSI. In fact, possessing these skills is why they engage in such projects in the first place.

The dynamics in SSI, where actors dynamically assume, leave, or change roles, can be explained using the S-D logic concept of service ecosystems with the project as an engagement platform (Lusch & Nambisan, 2015). The configurations of involved actors and their activities for recombining and creating resources change over time. This process leads to an emerging smart service system concept, which is a blueprint for a future configuration of actors and resources. Hence, the desired smart service system emerges from a service ecosystem that evolved through the engagement of the involved actors. The concept of ecosystem states distinguishes the realizing state, which roughly relates to the "development" from the outcoming state, which can be understood as "operations." However, the transition between these states is fluid and may not directly relate to traditional milestones such as "project start" and "service launch." From a macro-level perspective, SSI represents a state in the evolution of a service ecosystem.

An SDL-grounded theory of SSI can answer the call for midrange theories that link the meta-theoretical character of SDL with empirically accessible phenomena (Vargo & Lusch, 2017). It could establish a common ground to analyze and design the institutional arrangements that serve as an engagement platform for actors in different states of the service ecosystem. These institutional arrangements may also be used to conceptualize the embedding of SSE in projects and their development processes. Therefore, research objectives for establishing an SDL-grounded midrange theory of SSI may include the following:

- Identify and classify operant and operand resources in SSI, e.g., based on ecosystem roles.
- Identify the institutions that make up the institutional arrangement at the realizing state, e.g., projects, and at the outcoming state, e.g., service platforms.
- Identify actor engagement that can be classified as institutional work, e.g., agreement on jointly used methods, practices, and modeling notations to advance the project organization.
- Develop prescriptive knowledge, e.g., design principles, that guide the establishment of service ecosystems and their institutional arrangements for value co-creation.

References

Azkan, C., Iggena, L., Gür, I., Möller, F., & Otto, B. (2020a). A taxonomy for data-driven Services in Manufacturing Industries. In *24th Pacific Asia Conference on Information Systems.*

Azkan, C., Möller, F., Meisel, L., & Otto, B. (2020b). Service dominant logic perspective on data ecosystems-a case study based morphology. In *Twenty-Eighth European Conference on Information Systems.*

Beverungen, D., Lüttenberg, H., & Wolf, V. (2018). Recombinant service systems engineering. *Business and Information Systems Engineering, 60,* 377–391. https://doi.org/10.1007/s12599-018-0526-4

Beverungen, D., Müller, O., Matzner, M., Mendling, J., & Vom Brocke, J. (2019). Conceptualizing smart service systems. *Electronic Markets, 29,* 7–18. https://doi.org/10.1007/s12525-017-0270-5

Bland, D. J., Osterwalder, A., Smith, A., & Papadakos, T. (2019). *Testing business ideas. Strategyzer series.* John Wiley & Sons, Inc.

Böhmann, T., Leimeister, J. M., & Möslein, K. (2014). Service systems engineering. *Business and Information Systems Engineering, 6,* 73–79. https://doi.org/10.1007/s12599-014-0314-8

Böttcher, T. P., Rickling, L., Gmelch, K., Weking, J., & Krcmar, H. (2021). Towards the digital self-renewal of retail: The generic ecosystem of the retail industry. In *Wirtschaftsinformatik 2021 Proceedings. AIS Electronic Library (AISeL).*

Brogt, T., & Strobel, G. (2020). Service Systems in the era of the internet of things: A smart service system taxonomy. In *Twenty-Eighth European Conference on Information Systems.*

Brozović, D., & Tregua, M. (2022). The evolution of service systems to service ecosystems: A literature review. *International Journal of Management Reviews., 24,* 459. https://doi.org/10.1111/ijmr.12287

Brust, L., Breidbach, C., Antons, D., & Salge, T.-O. (2017). Service-dominant logic and information systems research: A review and analysis using topic modeling. In Y. J. Kim, R. Agarwal, & J. K. Lee (Eds.), *Proceedings of the International Conference on Information Systems–Transforming Society with Digital Innovation, ICIS 2017, Seoul, South Korea.* Association for Information Systems.

Clarke, P., & O'Connor, R. V. (2012). The situational factors that affect the software development process: Towards a comprehensive reference framework. *Information and Software Technology, 54,* 433–447. https://doi.org/10.1016/j.infsof.2011.12.003

Dedehayir, O., Mäkinen, S. J., & Roland Ortt, J. (2018). Roles during innovation ecosystem genesis: A literature review. *Technological Forecasting and Social Change, 136,* 18–29. https://doi.org/10.1016/j.techfore.2016.11.028

den Hertog, P. (2000). Knowledge-intensive business services as co-producers of innovation. *International Journal of Innovation Management., 04,* 491–528. https://doi.org/10.1142/S136391960000024X

Ehrenthal, J. C. F., Gruen, T. W., & Hofstetter, J. S. (2021). Recommendations for conducting service-dominant logic research. In R. Dornberger (Ed.), *New trends in business information systems and technology* (Vol. 294, pp. 281–297). Springer International Publishing.

Ekman, P., Raggio, R. D., & Thompson, S. M. (2016). Service network value co-creation: Defining the roles of the generic actor. *Industrial Marketing Management, 56,* 51–62. https://doi.org/10.1016/j.indmarman.2016.03.002

Floerecke, S., Lehner, F., & Schweikl, S. (2020). Cloud computing ecosystem model: Evaluation and role clusters. *Electronic Markets, 31,* 923. https://doi.org/10.1007/s12525-020-00419-2

Frank, M., Gausemeier, J., Hennig-Cardinal von Widdern, N., Koldewey, C., Menzefricke, J. S., & Reinhold, J. (2020). A reference process for the smart service business: Development and practical implications. In *ISPIM connects.* Partnering for an Innovative Community.

Gebauer, H., Paiola, M., Saccani, N., & Rapaccini, M. (2021). Digital servitization: Crossing the perspectives of digitization and servitization. *Industrial Marketing Management, 93,* 382–388. https://doi.org/10.1016/j.indmarman.2020.05.011

Giray, G., & Tekinerdogan, B. (2018). Situational method engineering for constructing internet of things development methods. In B. Shishkov (Ed.), *Business modeling and Software Design: 8th International Symposium, BMSD 2018, Vienna, Austria, Proceedings* (Vol. 319, pp. 221–239). Springer International Publishing.

Gottschalk, S., Yigitbas, E., Nowosad, A., & Engels, G. (2023). Continuous situation-specific development of business models: Knowledge provision, method composition, and method enactment. *Software and Systems Modeling, 22*, 47–73. https://doi.org/10.1007/s10270-022-01018-9

Hagen, S., Kammler, F., & Thomas, O. (2018). Adapting product-service system methods for the digital era: Requirements for smart PSS engineering. In S. Hankammer, K. Nielsen, F. T. Piller, G. Schuh, & N. Wang (Eds.), *Customization 4.0* (Vol. 97, pp. 87–99). Springer International Publishing.

Harmsen, F., Brinkkemper, S., & Oei, H. (1994). Situational method engineering for information system project approaches. In A. A. Verrijn-Stuart & T. W. Olle (Eds.), *Proceedings of the IFIP WG8.1 Working Conference on Methods and Associated Tools for the Information Systems Life Cycle*. Elsevier Science.

Hefnawy, A., Bouras, A., & Cherifi, C. (2016). IoT for Smart City services. In D. E. Boubiche, F. Hidoussi, L. Guezouli, A. Bounceur, & H. T. Cruz (Eds.), *ICC 2016: Proceedings of the International Conference on Internet of things and Cloud Computing* (pp. 1–9). ACM, Inc.

Henderson-Sellers, B., & Ralyté, J. (2010). Situational method engineering: State-of-the-art review. *Journal of Universal Computer Science, 16*, 424–478.

Holler, M., Herterich, M., Dremel, C., Uebernickel, F., & Brenner, W. (2018). Towards a method compendium for the development of digitised products–findings from a case study. *IJPLM, 11*, 131. https://doi.org/10.1504/IJPLM.2018.092825

Huber, R. X. R., Püschel, L. C., & Röglinger, M. (2019). Capturing smart service systems: Development of a domain-specific modelling language. *Information Systems Journal, 29*, 1207–1255. https://doi.org/10.1111/isj.12269

Jacobson, I., Ng, P. W., & Spence, I. (2007). Enough of processes–lets do practices. *Journal of Object Technology, 6*, 41. https://doi.org/10.5381/jot.2007.6.6.c5

Jacobson, I., Spence, I., & Ng, P.-W. (2017). Is there a single method for the internet of things? *Communications of the ACM, 60*, 46–53. https://doi.org/10.1145/3106637

Jalonen, H. (2012). The uncertainty of innovation: A systematic review of the literature. *Journal of Management Research, 4*, 1–47. https://doi.org/10.5296/jmr.v4i1.1039

Kaiser, C., Stocker, A., Viscusi, G., Fellmann, M., & Richter, A. (2021). Conceptualising value creation in data-driven services: The case of vehicle data. *International Journal of Information Management, 59*, 102335. https://doi.org/10.1016/j.ijinfomgt.2021.102335

Kuhrmann, M., Tell, P., Hebig, R., Klunder, J. A.-C., Munch, J., Linssen, O., Pfahl, D., Felderer, M., Prause, C., Macdonell, S., Nakatumba-Nabende, J., Raffo, D., Beecham, S., Tuzun, E., Lopez, G., Paez, N., Fontdevila, D., Licorish, S., Kupper, S., Ruhe, G., Knauss, E., Ozcan-Top, O., Clarke, P., Mc Caffery, F. H., Genero, M., Vizcaino, A., Piattini, M., Kalinowski, M., Conte, T., Prikladnicki, R., Krusche, S., Coskuncay, A., Scott, E., Calefato, F., Pimonova, S., Pfeiffer, R.-H., Pagh Schultz, U., Heldal, R., Fazal-Baqaie, M., Anslow, C., Nayebi, M., Schneider, K., Sauer, S., Winkler, D., Biffl, S., Bastarrica, C., & Richardson, I. (2021). What makes agile software development agile. *IIEEE Transactions on Software Engineering, 48*, 3523. https://doi.org/10.1109/TSE.2021.3099532

Lingens, B., Miehé, L., & Gassmann, O. (2021). The ecosystem blueprint: How firms shape the design of an ecosystem according to the surrounding conditions. *Long Range Planning, 54*, 102043. https://doi.org/10.1016/j.lrp.2020.102043

Lusch, R. F., & Nambisan, S. (2015). Service innovation: A service-dominant logic perspective. *MIS Quarterly, 39*, 155–175.

Lüttenberg, H. (2020). PS3–A domain-specific modeling language for platform-based smart service systems. In S. Hofmann, O. Müller, & M. Rossi (Eds.), *Designing for digital transformation.*

Co-creating services with citizens and industry (Vol. 12388, pp. 438–450). SPRINGER NATURE.

Martin, D., Kühl, N., & Maleshkova, M. (2020). Grasping the terminology: Smart services, smart service systems, and cyber-physical systems. In M. Maleshkova, N. Kühl, & P. Jussen (Eds.), *Smart service management: Design guidelines and best practices* (pp. 7–21). Springer.

Marx, E., Pauli, T., Fielt, E., & Matzner, M. (2020). From services to smart services: Can service engineering methods get smarter as well? In *15th International Conference on Wirtschaftsinformatik*.

Müller, P. (2013). *Integrated engineering of products and services: Layer-based development methodology for product-service systems*. Dissertation, Technische Universität.

Osterwalder, A., Pigneur, Y., Smith, A., & Etiemble, F. (2020). *The invincible company: Your're holding a guide to the world's best business models: Use it to inspire your own portfolio of new ideas and reinventions: Design a culture of innovation and transformation to become*. Wiley.

Pakkala, D., & Spohrer, J. (2019). Digital service: Technological Agency in Service Systems. In T. Bui (Ed.), *Proceedings of the 52nd Hawaii International Conference on System Sciences*. Hawaii International Conference on System Sciences.

Papert, M., & Pflaum, A. (2017). Development of an ecosystem model for the realization of internet of things (IoT) Services in Supply Chain Management. *Electronic Markets, 31*, 306. https://doi.org/10.1007/s12525-017-0251-8

Pfeiffer, A., Krempels, K.-H., & Jarke, M. (2017). Service-oriented business model framework–a service-dominant logic based approach for business modeling in the digital era. In *Proceedings of the 19th International Conference on Enterprise Information Systems* (pp. 361–372). SCITEPRESS–Science and Technology Publications.

Pirola, F., Boucher, X., Wiesner, S., & Pezzotta, G. (2020). Digital technologies in product-service systems: A literature review and a research agenda. *Computers in Industry, 123*, 103301. https://doi.org/10.1016/j.compind.2020.103301

Pöppelbuß, J., & Durst, C. (2019). Smart service canvas–A tool for analyzing and designing smart product-service systems. *Procedia CIRP, 83*, 324–329. https://doi.org/10.1016/j.procir.2019.04.077

Rapaccini, M., & Adrodegari, F. (2022). Conceptualizing customer value in data-driven services and smart PSS. *Computers in Industry, 137*, 103607. https://doi.org/10.1016/j.compind.2022.103607

Riasanow, T., Jäntgen, L., Hermes, S., Böhm, M., & Krcmar, H. (2020). Core, intertwined, and ecosystem-specific clusters in platform ecosystems: Analyzing similarities in the digital transformation of the automotive, blockchain, financial, insurance and IIoT industry. *Electronic Markets*. https://doi.org/10.1007/s12525-020-00407-6

Szopinski, D., Schoormann, T., John, T., Knackstedt, R., & Kundisch, D. (2019). Software tools for business model innovation: Current state and future challenges. *Electronic Markets, 60*, 469. https://doi.org/10.1007/s12525-018-0326-1

Tell, P., Klunder, J., Kupper, S., Raffo, D., MacDonell, S. G., Munch, J., Pfahl, D., Linssen, O., & Kuhrmann, M. (2019). What are hybrid development methods made of? An evidence-based characterization. In *2019 IEEE/ACM International Conference on Software and System Processes (ICSSP)* (pp. 105–114). IEEE.

Turetken, O., Grefen, P., Gilsing, R., & Adali, O. E. (2019). Service-dominant business model Design for Digital Innovation in smart mobility. *Business and Information Systems Engineering, 61*, 9–29. https://doi.org/10.1007/s12599-018-0565-x

Vargo, S. L., & Lusch, R. F. (2016). Institutions and axioms: An extension and update of service-dominant logic. *Journal of the Academy of Marketing Science, 44*, 5–23. https://doi.org/10.1007/s11747-015-0456-3

Vargo, S. L., & Lusch, R. F. (2017). Service-dominant logic 2025. *International Journal of Research in Marketing, 34*, 46–67. https://doi.org/10.1016/j.ijresmar.2016.11.001

Vink, J., Koskela-Huotari, K., Tronvoll, B., Edvardsson, B., & Wetter-Edman, K. (2021). Service ecosystem design: Propositions, process model, and future research agenda. *Journal of Service Research, 24*, 168–186. https://doi.org/10.1177/1094670520952537

Weiß, P., Zolnowski, A., Warg, M., & Schuster, T. (2018). Service dominant architecture: Conceptualizing the Foundation for Execution of digital strategies based on S-D logic. In T. Bui (Ed.), *Proceedings of the 51ˢᵗ Hawaii International Conference on System Sciences*. Hawaii International Conference on System Sciences.

Wellsandt, S., Cattaneo, L., Cerri, D., Terzi, S., Corti, D., Norden, C., & Ahlers, R. (2018). Life cycle management for product-service systems. In L. Cattaneo & S. Terzi (Eds.), *Models, methods and tools for product service design: The Manutelligence Project* (1st ed., pp. 29–43). Horizon 2020 Framework Programme.

Windasari, N. A., & Lin, F.-R. (2021). Explicating open innovation using service-dominant logic. *International Journal of Service Science, Management, Engineering, and Technology, 12*, 78–98. https://doi.org/10.4018/IJSSMET.2021030105

Wolf, V., Franke, A., Bartelheimer, C., & Beverungen, D. (2020). Establishing smart service systems is a challenge: A case study on pitfalls and implications. In N. Gronau, M. Heine, K. Poustcchi, & H. Krasnova (Eds.), *WI2020 Community Tracks* (pp. 103–119). GITO Verlag.

Zolnowski, A., Anke, J., & Gudat, J. (2017). Towards a cost-benefit-analysis of data-driven business models. In *Proceedings of the 13ᵗʰ International Conference on Wirtschaftsinformatik*.

Chapter 7
Conclusion

Smart service innovation is highly relevant in both practice and academia. While practitioners are keen to seize the potential of digital technologies for service innovation, they often struggle to design viable smart service systems successfully. Research in disciplines like information systems, marketing, industrial engineering, and innovation management has developed various principles, models, methods, languages, and tools that are (potentially) applicable to SSI. Understanding the characteristics of smart service innovation is the prerequisite for building on the foundation of existing means that could support the analysis, design, implementation, and management of smart services.

The presented research results contribute to the systematic development of smart service systems by advancing the understanding of smart service innovation through empirical insights into the structure, organization, and conduct of real-world SSI projects. The evidence provided in this book confirms previous research suggests that SSI projects are interdisciplinary multi-actor settings, which are beset with complexity and uncertainty. The involved actors apply a broad spectrum of methods from various disciplines and face various challenges in project management and service design. Based on the empirical findings, different conceptual results have been elaborated, e.g., to characterize the value propositions of actors using a set of roles, explain the dynamics of their involvement during the project using ecosystem states, and the activities they perform to reduce uncertainty in the innovation project. Additionally, typical constellations of actor-role-assignments have been conceptualized as innovation patterns. Conducting SSI projects based on suitable methods from different disciplines is the focus of service systems engineering. The presented results show the diversity of methods used in practice and how they can be combined suitably. The variety of work products resulting from the application of different methods makes it difficult to gain an overall understanding of the current state of the development. The Lifecycle Modeling Language is suitable to fulfill the needs of different stakeholders through its ability to integrate different perspectives of smart service systems into consistent views. Activities that ensure economic viability can reduce uncertainty but lack suitable methods. Therefore, meta-models, methods, and

J. Anke, *Smart Service Innovation*, SpringerBriefs in Information Systems,
https://doi.org/10.1007/978-3-031-43770-0_7

tools were developed to assess smart services and their business models already within the design process rather than at the end.

These findings progress the understanding of smart service innovation and serve as a foundation for improved methodologies and design theories, especially related to a better embedding service systems engineering into multi-actor service innovation. Practitioners can benefit from these results for the setup and conduct of their innovation projects and for strategic considerations of their capabilities, partnerships, and dependencies.

Further research can be expected to create design knowledge that guides practitioners in the challenging task of systematically designing smart service systems. This will help organizations exploit the potential of digital technologies to create innovative value propositions and gain a competitive advantage. On a larger scale, smart services may transform the way people interact with each other, create value, and improve their lives. The systematic investigation of these phenomena has just begun and will remain a fascinating topic for academics of multiple disciplines in the years to come.